GW00570309

CLASSIC SALMON FLIES
The Francis Francis Collection

FRANCIS FRANCIS AND HIS GILLIE

CLASSIC SALMON FLIES

THE FRANCIS FRANCIS COLLECTION

Described and illustrated by
JAMES WALTHAM

Adam and Charles Black · London

First published 1983
A & C Black (Publishers) Ltd
35 Bedford Row, London WC1R 4JH

ISBN 0-7136-2316-0

Waltham, James
Classic salmon flies.
1. Flies, Artificial
I. Title
688.7'912 SH451
ISBN 0-7136-2316-0

Typeset in Great Britain by August Filmsetting, Warrington, Cheshire.
Printed in Great Britain by R. J. Acford, Chichester, Sussex.

Contents

Note on the illustrations vii
Acknowledgements vii
Francis Francis: an appreciation viii

Chapter 1
General Flies 1

Chapter 2
Flies for Scottish Rivers
The Tweed 7
The Kirkcudbrightshire Dee 9
The Cree and its tributary, the Minnick 10
The Bladenoch 10
The Luce 10
The Ayrshire Stinchar 11
The Annan and Nith 11
The Aberdeenshire Dee 12
The Don 14
The Deveron 15
The Ness 15
The Garry of Loch Ness 18
The Conon 19
The Lochy 20
The Thurso 21
The Laxford 22
The Awe and the Orchy 23
The Shin 25
The Oykel 26
The Brora 27
The Helmsdale 28
The Beauly 28
The Findhorn 29
The Tay 32
The Tummel, Garry and Isla 35
The Lyon 36
The Earn 37
The Teith 38
The Forth 39
The Spey 40
Loch Lomond 41

Chapter 3
Flies for Irish Rivers and Loughs
The Erne 43
Lough Melvin 45
Lough Gill 46
The Moy 46
Lough Conn 48
The Owenmore and Ballycroy 49
Galway and Connemara 51
Lough Inchiquin 53
The Lennan and Lough Fern in Donegal 53
The Shannon 53
Killarney and the Flesk 55
The Laune 56
The Lee, Cork 57
The Cork Blackwater 59
The Bandon 60
The Caragh and Lough Currane 61
The Kerry Blackwater 62
The Suir 63
The Nore 64
The Bush 65
The Bann 67

Chapter 4

Flies for Welsh and English Rivers

The Usk 69
The Wye 71
The Dovey or Dyfi 72
The Conway 73
The Cothi 74
The Taff 75
The Tivey or Teifi, and Towy 76
The Dee 78
The Esk (Border) 78
The Eden 79
The Lune 81
The Ribble and Hodder 82
The Tyne 83
The Taw and Torridge 84

Appendix A

How to Dress a Salmon Fly 86

Appendix B

Feathers and Substitutes 99

A full index of all the patterns named in the text is printed on pages 111–16.

Note on the illustrations

Of the several hundred patterns listed in this book forty are illustrated in colour (between pages 68–69).

A further fifty-one patterns are illustrated in the text, and a key to all those illustrated is given in the complete index of patterns printed on pages 111–16.

For the benefit of the inexperienced fly-tyer a diagrammatic illustration, 'The Parts of a Salmon Fly' precedes the text (page xii) and Appendix A (How to Dress a Salmon Fly) is fully illustrated with descriptive drawings to show all stages of construction.

Acknowledgements

I would like to acknowledge the help and guidance given to me by my publishers, and to thank the many friends who encouraged me in the preparation of this book. Special thanks are due to my old chum and fellow angler, Howard Heaton, and I am grateful to Terry Eams of Partridge Hooks for sending me so much information, often at short notice.

Finally, and most particularly, my thanks go to my wife Heather for her patient long-suffering while her house was littered with manuscript and pieces of artwork and her ears were tormented by the constant click of the typewriter.

Francis Francis: An Appreciation

The latter years of the nineteenth century and the early part of the twentieth century have appropriately been described by angling writer and fly tying expert T. Donald Overfield as the 'Flamboyant Era' of salmon fly design and dressing. Not only were the French Impressionists able to demonstrate to the world a new sense of freedom and expression, for the same era, albeit less known, produced other masters of their craft who with cunning dexterity blended fur and feather into beautiful, and often exotic, works of art to delight the eye of both angler and fish alike. It is little wonder that the traditional salmon flies of this period were, and still are, so collectable and prized.

Over the past fifty years or so the salmon fly has undergone a number of changes. Double and treble hooks are now in vogue, while in general, salmon flies have become increasingly smaller and more simple in design. Moreover, with the exception of a few of the more famous patterns, they have taken on a more sombre appearance. Gone are the colourful jointed bodies, and the once delicate wings of married feathers have been replaced by animal fibres. Although no-one could ever doubt the ability of the modern fly to take fish, it nevertheless seems somehow regrettable that so much of the art and skill developed by the old masters became laid aside – the abstract for the classical.

Despite these changes in fashion, all is not lost. Over the past decade fly-tying has become an increasingly popular recreation now enjoyed by thousands of devotees the world over. More encouraging has been the recent resurgence of interest in the fly patterns of yesteryear. Once more students of the art are studying the teachings of the early professors and are re-discovering the pleasure and satisfaction which creating these flamboyant gems can bring.

Possibly the most enthusiastic collector of these traditional flies was author, editor, angling expert and fish culturist Francis Francis who listed his collection of flies for all the major British salmon rivers in his classic work *A Book on Angling*, first published in 1867 and subsequently revised in a number of later editions. Most of the flies given in this unique collection are the original designs of their inventors, some of whom are legends to this day. These were men who combined their love for fishing with fly-tying in a life-long search for the ideal fly for their favourite rivers. Irrespective of their social status, Francis sought the company of these master craftsmen and enjoyed countless blissful days fishing with them in every part of the United Kingdom. Those whose skills he was unable to study, Francis wasted no time in writing to them to procure their individual inventions. And so over many years this collection, which is the subject matter for this book, was accumulated. I have tried as far as possible to set out the patterns in such a way that the modern fly-tyer will follow with ease. In addition, for its intrinsic value, I have included Francis's notes on the listed rivers along with letters which he received from his fellow anglers and fly-tyers. In producing this book my hope is that the reader will derive as many pleasurable hours spent tying these patterns as I myself have enjoyed. My thanks to Francis Francis, a truly great angler and writer who gave the angling world so much.

Francis Francis was born in 1822 at Seaton in Devonshire, the son of Captain Morgan, R.N., his mother being the only daughter of Mr Hartley, who founded the Hartley Institution at Southampton. He changed his name on coming of age and inheriting property. After being educated at various private schools, and with several tutors, he adopted the profession of a civil engineer, but on completing his articles abandoned it for sport and sporting literature. In 1851 he married Mary Cole of Oxford, and henceforth, happy in his domestic life, enthusiastically devoted himself to angling and all connected with it. No kind of fishing, from gudgeon to salmon, came amiss to him, and he speedily made himself familiar with every mode of catching fish. His ardour never flagged; a lifetime of fishing found him, when he reeled up his last line at Houghton, Hampshire, as enthusiastic as when in his boyhood he caught his first fish. He was angling editor of *The Field* for more than a quarter of a century, and frequently wrote his experiences as an angler, together with reminiscences of angling literature, and papers on cognate subjects in the columns of that newspaper. He found time also to make himself a fair classical scholar, and to obtain a knowledge of the masterpieces of the English language. The collection of a good angling library formed a congenial entertainment to him. Francis established the Thames Rights Defence Association, throughout life advocating the cause of fish culture, and suggested the plan of 'The National Fish-Culture Association' which was later carried out. He had a large share also in introducing the ova of English trout to the New Zealand and Tasmanian streams. Francis was a member of the commission on oyster culture from 1868 to 1870, and was always enthusiastic about the improvement of English streams. As naturalist director for some years of the Brighton Aquarium he had special opportunities for observing fish and making experiments on their culture.

He was a man of fine stature, active in mind and body, quick with his pen, and never unemployed; cheerful, bright, sympathetic, and independent, his courage was extraordinary, and was well exhibited in the indomitable fortitude with which he bore the pains and necessary operations of the attempts to cure the cancer in his tongue. Scrupulously fair in word and thought, his nervous temperament at times caused him to be hasty both in temper and judgment, but he was always ready to admit his mistakes, and was quick to forgive as well as to forget.

Thus he occupied himself with his rod and pen during many happy years until he was seized with a severe stroke of paralysis in 1883. Though he eventually recovered from this, he grew thinner month by month, from the cancer for which he had previously undergone two operations. He died in his chair on 24th December 1886, and was buried at Twickenham.

On the Test and Itchen, and on the Scottish Lochs and rivers which he loved to frequent, his name will long be remembered. His memory is the memory of a man who spent his life in contributing largely to the amusement of others.

JAMES WALTHAM 1982

(Information from the *Dictionary of National Biography* and other papers.)

For Heather, Susan, and Christopher

There are many persons who hold that half-a-dozen flies are enough to kill salmon on any river in the kingdom and who will despise the notion of such an extended list of flies. To such irreverent scoffers and heretical unbelievers I have nothing to say. Let them indulge in their répertoire *of a bit of old turkey carpet and a live barn-door rooster. They are, to the artists who attain eminence in the delightful occupation I have endeavoured to illustrate, what the chalker of pavements is to a Landseer. Equally well, no doubt, would they land a salmon if they hooked him with a clothes-prop, a jack-line, and a meat hook.*

FRANCIS FRANCIS

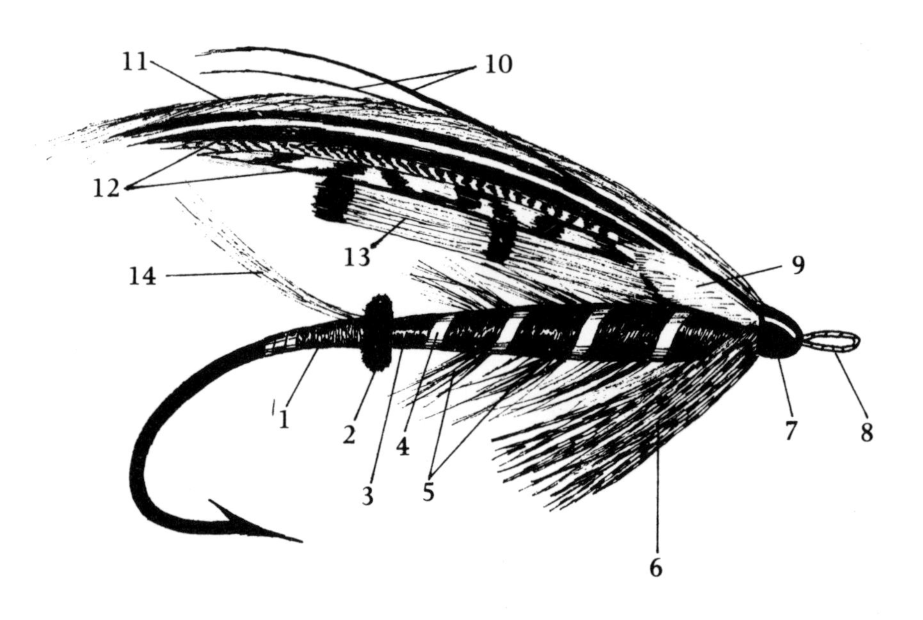

THE PARTS OF A SALMON FLY

1 Tag
2 Butt
3 Body
4 Rib
5 Hackle (body)
6 Shoulder (or throat hackle)
7 Head
8 Eye, or loop
9 Cheeks
10 Horns
11 Topping
12 Wings (or over wing)
13 Under (or inner) wing
14 Tail

Chapter One

General Flies

These are flies which have proved to be killers on any river. All hook sizes are given in the old Limerick scale. (See Appendix A.)

The Blue Doctor *Colour plate 1*

This is a very general and deserved favourite – one of the most general favourites we have, in fact.

Tag Commencing at the bend of the hook, tie on as a tag three or four turns of fine gold twist.

Tail A single golden pheasant topping (crest feather).

Butt A turn of scarlet crewel (a worsted yarn used in fancywork).

Body Pale blue floss silk.

Rib Silver tinsel. (In large flies of all kinds, the tinsel may be rendered more conspicuous by the addition of some twist wound on beside it.)

Hackle A shade darker than the body, wound on from tail to head; this is varied at times with blue jay's feather, or alternatively a spotted guinea fowl (gallina) breast or flank feather dyed blue can be used as a substitute for blue jay. (See Appendix B.)

Shoulder A brown grouse, partridge or bustard hackle.

Wings The wing is a mixed one containing fibres of bustard, dark turkey, argus pheasant, and claret, blue and yellow fibres of stained swan feathers, the latter predominating. In smaller flies mallard and pintail are introduced.

Head The head is of a scarlet crewel.

Hooks 6–10

The Silver Doctor

Tag Silver tinsel.

Tail A golden pheasant topping.

Butt A turn of red crewel.

Body Silver tinsel.

Hackle Blue, same shade as Blue Doctor.

Shoulder Brown hackle and a small speckled gallina (guinea fowl).

Wings Chiefly of pintail with a few red and blue swan fibres and two toppings over it.

Head Red crewel.

Hooks 6–10

And a very pretty showy fly it makes.

Having finished with the medical profession, we now turn to the army, and produce . . .

The Colonel *Colour plate 1*

This fly rejoices in two uniforms: the one a bright gold or yellow, and the other a red gold, or orange.

Tag Gold twist and two turns of bright yellow floss.

Tail Red and yellow sprigs (swan) mixed with gallina and topping.

Body Yellow floss half-way up, and then orange pig's wool.

Rib Gold twist, tinsel and black floss (a bit of unravelled coarse sewing silk does better) – first the twist, then the tinsel, then the black silk.

Hackle Yellow from tail to head.
Shoulder Bustard. (The grey, and oak brown speckled feathers from the wing of the turkey make good substitutes.)
Wings For the under part of the wing use two golden pheasant tippets tied back to back. The over wing: strips of pheasant (the small speckled feather); fibres of yellow thrown in here and there, and over all a topping.
Horns Blue macaw.
Head Black.
Hooks 4–8 to suit the water.

For the orange variety read orange for yellow.

The Major

This is a capital fly, but I think some of the dressing is over-done and might be dispensed with.

Tag Silver tinsel and ruby floss.
Tail Fibres of bustard hackle, tippet (the barred orange collar feather of a golden pheasant) and a topping.
Body Composite, viz. two turns of medium blue, ditto of dark orange wool, about four or five turns of bright claret, and two more of blue pig's wool: the latter picked out in longish fibres at the shoulder. (Use seal's fur as a substitute for pig's wool.)
Rib Silver tinsel and gold twist side by side.
Hackle A red claret hackle commencing from the orange.
Shoulder A bustard hackle and over this a yellow hackle.
Wings A white ribbed snipe's feather, with longish tippet on either side, over this bustard and golden pheasant tail in strips, with red, blue and greenish-yellow swan fibres, and over all a topping.
Head Black.
Hooks 4–8

Following up the military lead, we come to the list of Rangers.

The Black Ranger

Tag Silver twist and golden floss.
Tail The bright red breast feather of Indian crow and a topping.
Butt Two turns of black ostrich herl.
Body Two or three turns of golden floss, the same of bright fiery-red pig's wool and the remainder of black pig's wool.
Rib Silver tinsel and twist.
Hackle Very dark blue extending from the red part of the body.
Shoulder Black hackle.
Wings A pair of long jungle-cock feathers, a trifle longer than the hook with doubled tippet feathers over them and a topping over all.
Cheeks Kingfisher.
Horns Blue macaw.
Head Black.
Hooks 4–10 to suit the water.

The Blue Ranger

Tag Silver twist and gold-coloured floss.
Tail The bright red breast feather of an Indian crow and a topping.
Butt Black ostrich herl.
Body Gold-coloured floss and fiery-red pig's wool (as before) and light blue pig's wool for the rest of the body.
Rib Silver tinsel and twist.
Hackle Blue hackle, a shade darker than the body commencing from almost the middle of the wool to the shoulder.
Shoulder Gallina.
Wings A pair of tippets with double jungle-cock over them and a topping over all.
Head Black.
Hooks 4–10

We will now leave the military and go into the church.

The Parson *Colour plate 1*

This is a very showy fly and is used chiefly on the Erne, but it is a capital fly anywhere where a showy fly is required. It is on the Erne that we have a series of parsons, and we have there, green parsons, blue parsons, and golden parsons, and so on; the parson being merely significant of plenty of toppings in the wing. The golden parson, however, is my idea of the fly and this I will describe.

Tag	Silver tinsel and mauve floss.
Tail	Two toppings, a few sprigs of tippet and a kingfisher feather.
Butt	Black ostrich herl.
Body	Two turns of gold-coloured floss, then golden pig's wool merging into orange.
Rib	Silver twist.
Hackle	Golden orange hackle over the wool with red orange hackle over that. Two or three toppings are tied in at the breast instead of a shoulder hackle.
Wings	A tippet feather with a cock of the rock (not the squared feather) on either side and as many toppings as you can pile on – seven or eight, or more if you like.
Cheeks	Kingfisher.
Horns	Blue macaw.
Head	Black.
Hooks	4–10 to suit the water.

At Ballyshannon, the parson is often tied with the toppings turned upwards and this gives the fly more play in the water. This, however, is decidedly a *topping* parson, a sort of bishop or archbishop parson, in fact, and not for everyday use. We only bring him out when the feelings of the salmon, having resisted all ordinary persuasiveness, require to be very strongly appealed to. But if you substitute a golden olive hackle, with a medium claret above that, and a blue jay at the shoulder, no breast toppings, and reduce the number of toppings in the wing, and tie into the wing a couple of golden pheasant saddle feathers over the tippet feather, a capital working parson – a sort of curate – is produced, fit for hard everyday work.

We now come to the *bourgeois* and begin with one whose very name is ensanguined.

The Butcher *Colour plate 1*

This fly kills almost wherever there are salmon. In the Awe, the Orchy, the Brora, the Naver, the Thurso, the Helmsdale, the Annan, and the Taw and Torridge and one or two Welsh rivers. It is a prime favourite; in fact it kills well all over the kingdom and almost all over the world.

Tag	Gold twist and orange floss.
Tail	One topping.
Butt	Black ostrich herl.
Body	Red, medium blue, red, and blue pig's wool in equal portions.
Rib	Broad silver tinsel.
Hackle	Medium red claret.
Shoulder	Gallina.
Wings	Under wing, a pair of tippets (back to back) covered by a pair of golden pheasant rump feathers. Over them strips of brown mallard, bustard, peacock wing, wood-duck and blue and yellow strips of swan. (Mandarin duck can be used as substitute for wood-duck, sometimes referred to as summer-duck.)
Head	Black.
Hooks	4–10

Here is another plan of dressing the fly sent to me by a friend who is a very skilful brother of the craft, being no less than the gentleman who used to write those chatty articles in *Bell's Life*, under the *nom de plume* of 'Fin'. I give his own directions:

Fin's Butcher

Tag	Gold twist and orange floss.
Tail	Topping and wood-duck.
Butt	Black ostrich herl.
Body	Claret, blue, and orange pig's wool in equal portions.
Rib	Three turns of broad silver twist.
Hackle	Light claret.
Shoulder	Dark claret.
Wings	As before, with long jungle-cock feathers at sides.
Cheeks	Small kingfisher feathers.
Head	Black.
Hooks	4–10

The Baker

This is another good general fly; dressed small it is a standard fly on the Dovey.

Tag Gold twist and lightish blue floss.
Tail A topping.
Butt Black ostrich herl.
Body Gold-coloured floss, then dark orange, light blue, and red pig's wool in equal portions.
Rib Broadish gold tinsel.
Hackle Medium red claret.
Shoulder Gallina with light blue over it.
Wings Under wings, two tippet feathers (back to back). Over, sprigs of golden pheasant tail, bustard, peacock, red, bright green, blue, and yellow sprigs of swan.
Horns Blue macaw.
Head Black.
Hooks 4–10

Having given the butcher and the baker, the trades would not be complete without the following fly.

The Candlestick Maker

This is a fly to light the salmon to bed with. I dressed one as a whim some years since and sent it to a friend who reported favourably of it to me. Since then it has done useful service. At dusk this fly will often show the salmon the way upstairs when others will fail.

Tag Silver tinsel.
Tail Scarlet ibis and wood-duck.
Body The lower half is black silk then black pig's wool, very bushy towards the shoulder and picked out at the breast.
Rib Broad silver tinsel.
Hackle Golden olive.
Shoulder Claret hackle.
Wings Five or six toppings with double jungle-cock on either side.
Hooks Various sizes to suit the water.

The Childers

This is another excellent general fly which is a slaughterer on the Thurso, the Naver, the Helmsdale, and the Brora.

Tag Gold twist and gold-coloured floss.
Tail A topping, some teal and tippet.
Body Yellow, orange, and dark red (somewhat of a lake) pig's wool in equal sections.
Rib Broad gold tinsel.
Hackle Dark red claret.
Shoulder Light blue hackle.
Wings Broad strips of whitish tipped dark turkey and strips of bustard and golden pheasant tail over it, mixed with slices of blue, pale red, orange, and yellow swan.
Head Black.
Hooks 4–10

The Claret

This fly may be varied by altering the shade of the claret which may be from light red to dark purple claret, the wing being sobered down as the fly is made darker. It is a very useful fly and a general favourite. It may be made of almost any size from 4 to 10 or even 11. It is good for sea-trout if dressed of the right size.

Tag Gold twist and gold floss.
Tail A topping.
Butt Black ostrich herl.
Body Three turns of orange floss, the rest medium reddish claret pig's wool.
Rib Stoutish gold thread.
Hackle Light reddish claret commencing about half-way down the body.
Shoulder Two or three turns of black hackle.
Wings Two tippet feathers (back to back) and mixed fibres of golden pheasant tail, turkey, bustard, and peacock over with fibres of green and red parrot thrown in, and one topping over all.
Horns Blue macaw.
Head Black.
Hooks 4–11 to suit the water.

The Black and Teal

This is my own pattern for dressing the larger version of this fly and a very good fly I consider it to be. The fly is a first-rate general fly and should be kept of all sizes as it will kill large lake and river trout or sea-trout, as well as salmon, if regulated in size. The smaller patterns may be made with single jungle-cock feathers, a trifle more teal being added. It is one of the best flies that can be used on the Spey and Tay. Some persons, however, dress it purely with a teal wing; it is good anyhow.

Tag	Silver twist and golden floss.
Tail	A topping.
Butt	Black ostrich herl.
Body	A few turns of orange floss, the rest black (either floss, horsehair, mohair, or unlaid sewing silk); in large flies fur is often used.
Rib	Broadish silver tinsel.
Hackle	Black over three parts of the body.
Shoulder	Gallina (the dark feather with the large round spots, not the small speckled grey).
Wings	Double jungle-cock with a topping over them and two good-sized teal, or slices of widgeon or pintail to form a body to the wing.
Head	Gold thread.
Hooks	3–12 to suit the water.

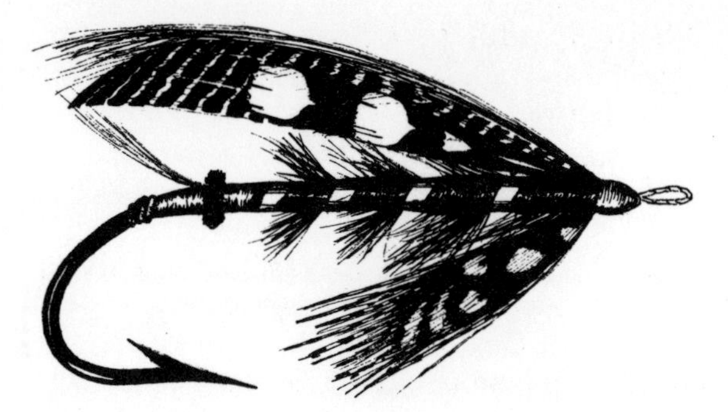

The Black and Teal

The Namsen

There is not a prettier body than the Namsen boasts of. It is a great favourite of mine.

Tag	Silver twist.
Tail	One topping with some red parrot and pintail sprigs.
Body	Dressed roughish, starting with a few turns of bright yellow pig's wool merging into deep orange and then into medium red claret, then again into bright medium to darkish blue. The upper part of the claret and the blue is tied in very roughly for picking out, the blue the longest, of course.
Rib	Silver tinsel with gold thread beside it.
Shoulder	Longish black hackle. (No body hackle.)
Wings	Slips of dark turkey, bright bustard, bittern wing, red, blue and greenish dyed swan.
Head	Black.
Hooks	4–10

The Popham *Colour plate 1*

This is a peculiar species of fly which kills upon two or three rivers in the North – I believe on the Ness and the Brora, and occasionally elsewhere. It never was a great favourite of mine, being a very troublesome fly to tie. It is, however, an established favourite with some anglers, and therefore I describe it.

Tag	Gold twist.
Tail	A topping.
Butt	Two turns of peacock herl.
Body	The body is in three joints; the lowest is yellow, the middle one orange and the upper one blue floss. At each joint there is a turn or two of peacock herl, and pointing downwards like hackles are three or four of the small red feathers from the breast of an Indian crow.
Rib	Fine gold twist.
Shoulder	Blue jay hackle.
Wings	Mixed fibres of golden pheasant tail and tippet, bustard, teal, blue, yellow, and claret-dyed swan, and a topping over all.
Head	Peacock herl.
Hooks	7–11

The Britannia

This is a very rich fly, but it is a tried, accepted favourite upon many rivers. It kills well on the

Thurso, to which river, by the way, I first introduced it several years ago. I had very good sport with it there.

Tag	Gold twist.
Tail	A good-sized topping, a bit of scarlet ibis and fibres of florican bustard.
Body	Two or three turns of bright golden floss, and then bright orange pig's wool.
Rib	Gold tinsel and silver twist.
Hackle	Bright red claret with bustard or wood-duck hackle over it.
Shoulder	Blue or green hackle tied rather as a ruff over the wing.
Wings	Two shovel duck feathers, with from three to five toppings over and two short jungle-cock at the sides.
Cheeks	Kingfisher.
Head	Gold thread.
Hooks	4, 5 or 6

A warm gorgeous-looking fly. By using a dark orange or a red-brown hackle, the warmth of the fly may be toned down. The green shoulder-hackled fly is my favourite.

The Goldfinch

A very showy, striking fly rather like the Canary.

Tag	Gold tinsel and black floss.
Tail	A topping.
Body	Gold-coloured floss.
Rib	Gold tinsel.
Hackle	Pale yellow.
Shoulder	Blue jay.
Wings	Composed entirely of toppings.
Horns	Red macaw.
Head	Black.
Hooks	5–7

Chapter Two

Flies for Scottish Rivers

TWEED FLIES

Few rivers are so varied in their character as the Tweed, which comprises in its length every kind of water – rapid, dub, stream and fall. The lower part of the salmon fishing is mostly boat-fishing but higher up it can be fished a good deal from the shore. The waters or holdings are not generally extensive, being very valuable and fetching high rents. The flies used are not large, and the sport runs from February to the end of November. For close information see a capital little work by Younger, published by Rutherford of Kelso, wherein every water and cast on the Tweed is named and described.

The Durham Ranger *Colour plate 2*
This is a favourite pattern on the Tweed, but it is, like most of the Tweed flies, good anywhere.

Tag Silver tinsel and gold floss.
Tail One topping.
Butt Black ostrich herl.
Body Two turns of light orange floss, then two of dark orange, two more turns of claret pig's wool, the rest black pig's wool picked out at the breast. The turns may of course be increased or lessened according to the size of the fly.
Rib Silver twist and tinsel.
Hackle Beginning at the wool, a coch-y-bonddu hackle (red with black centre) stained a bright red-orange, then two turns of black hackle over it.
Shoulder A bright blue hackle.
Wings A pair of longish jungle-cock with double tippets on either side. One topping over all.
Cheeks Kingfisher.
Horns Blue macaw.
Head Black.
Hooks 3–10 (the smaller sizes being better on the Tweed).

Jock Scott *Colour plate 2*
This is a peculiar fly and the only one of its sort, but it is a first-rate killer. It is another good Tweed fly, and is one of the most useful general flies we have elsewhere.

Tag Gold twist.
Tail A topping and an Indian crow feather.
Butt Black ostrich herl.
Body The body is in two joints – gold-coloured floss the lower and black floss the upper. From the joint is tied two or three short toucan points veiling over the gold joint and over the butts of them, at the joint, two turns of black ostrich (as a second butt). A topping dyed red can be used as a substitute for toucan.
Rib Silver twist.
Hackle Black hackle over the black joint.
Shoulder Speckled gallina.
Wings A white-tipped turkey slip in the middle then fibres of pintail or teal, bustard, brown mallard, yellow, red and green parrot and a topping over all. Green peacock herl can be included as an optional extra.

Cheeks Jungle cock.
Horns Blue macaw.
Head Black.
Hooks 6–11

The Dun Wing

Another capital Tweed favourite, which is a pretty general one also. It is one of the old Scottish patterns. This fly is a general favourite on the Kirkcudbrightshire Dee, the Annan and Nith; and, dressed on a long large hook it is good on the Tay and many other streams besides.

Tail A topping and sprigs of tippet.
Body Light orange, red claret, darkish blue, and black pig's wool in equal portions merging into each other. A few fibres of the blue wool picked out at the breast.
Rib Broadish silver tinsel.
Hackle Black hackle from the red wool to the shoulder.
Wings Two strips from the dun brown feather sometimes found in the tail of a turkey.
Head Black.
Hooks 5–10

The Drake Wing

This is another good Tweed fly, and a fair general favourite also.

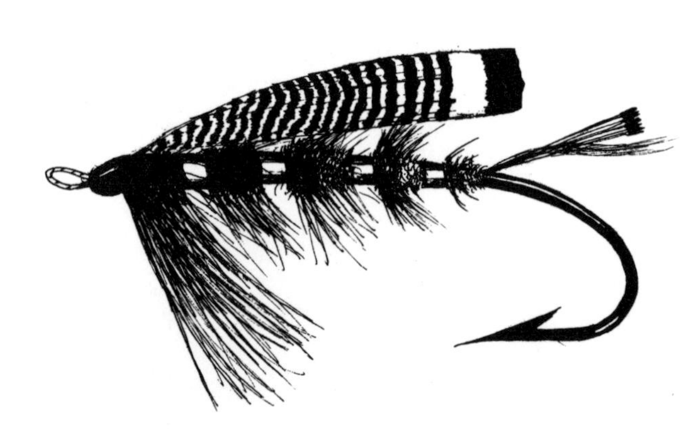

The Drake Wing

Tail Tippet sprigs and a yellow toucan feather.
Body Orange, red and black pig's wool, the black being about three-fifths of the body.
Rib Broadish silver tinsel.
Hackle A coch-y-bonddu hackle stained a dark orange red.
Shoulder A lavender hackle over the body hackle.
Wings Two strips of pintail or wood duck.
Head Black.
Hooks 6–11

The small edition of this fly, used in the summer, is called the Teal Wing, teal being substituted for pintail.

The White Wing

This fly I have never seen save on the Tweed. It is a capital fly for the evening there and kills well.

Tail One topping and a bit of tippet.
Body One turn of yellow, one of orange, one of claret, and the rest of black pig's wool.
Rib Broad silver tinsel.
Hackle Black from tail to head.
Shoulder Light blue hackle.
Wings Two strips of white swan.
Head Black.
Hooks 4, 5 or 6

The White Tip

This is like the last in every particular, save that there is no orange in the body, and the wings are two slips of the feather from a wild duck's wing with white tip and butt, and black in the middle.

Hooks 5–8

The Toppy

A noted old Tweed fly.

Tag Ruby floss.
Tail A tuft of yellow mohair.
Body Black pig's wool.
Rib Fine silver tinsel.

Hackle Two turns of red hackle by the tail and black hackle over the rest of the body to the shoulder.
Wings Two strips of dark turkey tipped with white.
Head Red mohair.
Hooks 5–8

The Black and Yellow

This is another capital fly, a first-rate general evening fly anywhere.

Tag Silver twist and orange floss.
Tail A topping or two according to the size of the fly.
Butt Black ostrich herl.
Body Black floss silk.
Rib Silver tinsel (if dressed large, twist with it).
Hackle Black.
Shoulder Light blue hackle.
Wings A red feather from a golden pheasant rump and the remainder of the wing composed of toppings according to the size and requirement of the fly, from three to seven or eight.
Cheeks Kingfisher.
Horns Blue macaw.
Head Black.
Hooks 6–11

The Wilkinson

Tag Silver thread and gold floss.
Tail A topping and a short stump of tippet.
Butt Red crewel.
Body Silver tinsel.
Rib Silver twist.
Hackle Medium blue.
Shoulder A bright lake hackle.
Wings A mixed wing of bustard, wood-duck, pintail, blue and red macaw, and a pair of jungle-cocks at the sides. One topping over all.
Cheeks Kingfisher.
Head Black.
Hooks 3–11

Sir Richard *Colour plate 2*

Tag Silver thread and gold floss.
Tail A topping and a short stump of tippet.
Butt Black ostrich herl.
Body Black floss.
Rib Broad silver tinsel and thread.
Shoulder A gallina hackle with blue jay over it (no body hackle).
Wings As the Wilkinson with a sprig of golden pheasant tail, black partridge, and tippet let in. No jungle-cock.
Head Black.
Hooks 3–11

Some of the Tay flies, particularly the Wasps, dressed small, will kill well in the Tweed. The above patterns are nearly all from the *repertoire* of my old acquaintance James Wright, of Sprouston, a first-rate artist. Beloe of Coldstream, and Forrest of Kelso, are also excellent furnishers of angling requisites. Forrest has a high name as a salmon rod maker, and Beloe is celebrated for his trout flies. For a salmon fly, however, James has deservedly 'the call' on Tweedside. Tweed flies range in size from medium sized salmon down to sea-trout size. The latter are tied on double hooks, which are very effective. The gayer flies certainly have the call, and Wilkinson, Jock Scott, and the Durham Ranger, with the Blue Doctor, are the most powerful persuaders plied upon Tweed; the old dun wings and drakes going more out of request. I shall keep them on the roll however, as now and then they come in.

THE KIRCUDBRIGHTSHIRE DEE

The Cree flies below will also kill on the Dee, as will the dun wing Tweed flies; but the favourite fly, given to me by Mr Laurie, of Laurieston, an old resident and renter of fishing in that river, is:

Tail A small topping.
Body Two turns of yellow and the rest of black pig's wool.
Rib Silver tinsel.
Hackle Black, to shoulder.

Wings	Two slips of swallow-tailed gled (kite).
Head	Black.
Hooks	These flies are not large, the ordinary grilse size and smaller (7–12).

THE CREE AND ITS TRIBUTARY, THE MINNICK

These are both good spring rivers.
Sir Herbert Maxwell, of Monreith, has sent me an account of the Wigton rivers, with patterns of flies; and his remarks are so clear and to the purpose that I append them. Here are his patterns:

No. 1

Tail	A tuft of red parrot and a topping.
Body	Yellow orange pig's wool merging into scarlet for half the body. The upper half black pig's wool dressed roughish.
Rib	Thin gold tinsel, doubled.
Hackle	Brown red.
Shoulder	Plenty of black hackle.
Wings	Turkey dun with lightish tips.
Head	Black.
Hooks	8–12

No. 2
The tail, body, tinsel and body hackle, as before. Shoulder hackle lightish medium blue. Wing slips of brown mallard.

No. 3
Tail and rib as before. Body dark cinnamon brown (darker than cinnamon); hackle the same shade. Shoulder hackle black; wing, brown mallard.

These are the standard flies, sizes from 8 to 12 in your Limerick scale. They are varied, and I think improved by a topping over, or a small tippet feather in the wing. The fish are numerous but small; most weigh about 10 lbs. The Butchers and Doctors kill well, and small dark Clarets.

THE BLADENOCH

A fair spring river, but at no season as good as the Cree, and the fish are very shy. The same flies will kill well dressed larger, but the favourite is the Dun Wing as dressed by Wright of Sprouston (see p. 8). Sizes from 4 to 6 in spring, down to 9 or 10 in summer. In spring the Butcher is also a prime favourite.

THE LUCE

This is a late river, but the fish run far heavier than in the Cree and Bladenoch, a 20 lb fish being by no means a rarity. Sir Herbert Maxwell's favourite flies for the Luce are as follows:

No. 1

Tag	Gold tinsel.
Tail	Red parrot, teal, and yellow macaw.
Body	Yellow, orange, scarlet and claret pig's wool, dressed spare.
Rib	Double gold thread.
Shoulder	Grouse hackle (no body hackle).
Wings	Red wild turkey and a topping over.
Head	Black.
Hooks	6–10

Another good one is a claret body with blue hackle on shoulder, grey mallard wing, or teal for small sizes.
Sir Herbert writes, 'The following eccentricity is reckoned excellent as a change and I know it does good work'.

No. 2

Tag	Gold tinsel.
Tail	A topping.
Body	Half yellow and half pea-green pig's wool, dressed spare.
Rib	Gold tinsel.
Hackle	Green hackle over green pig's wool.
Shoulder	Grouse.
Wings	Brown mallard, between which is a bright blue hackle. A topping over.

Head Black ostrich herl.
Hooks 8–9

About as ugly a fly as you will find.

The upper waters of the Cree and the Minnick are protected, but the lower and better part is netted. The Bladenoch is preserved by an association, but the Luce is terribly netted; the fish slaps are sometimes built up, and in short a general state of neglect and ignorance of what is law prevails. As to the stake netting in the Solway, into which these rivers debouch, I need not tell *you* that the Scotch shore fairly bristles with nets; it is a marvel fish get through and up at all.

There are other streams in Ayrshire and up the West coast, which have their peculiar flies; but were you to notice all these rivers, your book would swell to two or three volumes on salmon alone, which I presume is not your intention.

Herbert E. Maxwell

Sir Herbert has kindly subsequently sent me the following: . . . Add to the Minnick flies for low bright water the following, known as:

The Dusty Miller

Tag Silver tinsel and dark olive floss.
Tail One topping.
Butt Black ostrich herl.
Body Embossed silver tinsel.
Rib Gold thread.
Hackle Dark olive.
Shoulder Gallina.
Wings Golden pheasant tail, mallard, teal, green parrot and lavender swan.
Cheeks Jungle-cock.
Head Black.
Hooks 9–11

Subsequently this has become a capital general fly.

THE AYRSHIRE STINCHAR

This is a fine water; if the nets were off, I doubt not it would be the best in the West. The nets are, I believe, to be regulated in future by the proprietor, Lord Stair, a keen fisher. I have never fished it, but he told me the other day he had four fish weighing 76 lbs. Large Dee flies are used there, and a curious dun turkey, with a second pair of wings half way down the body. This plan is common on the Tay, and is employed when very long hooks are used, and when the fly-dresser has not any feathers by him long enough in the fibre to make the wing. He then takes two short fibres, and by allowing one to overlap the other the requisite effect is produced.

Mr J. Dalrymple Hay has sent me the following pattern which is a different tying of the Drake Wing and is thus described:

Drake Wing (2) (light)

Red and black body, with brown hackle; the wing can be of pintail or lighter mallard feathers.

THE ANNAN AND NITH

The following four patterns for the Annan were sent to me by Mr Rowell, the fishing-tackle maker of St Alban's Row, Carlisle. They are nicely tied and look decidedly bloodthirsty, being dressed roughish and without heads.

No. 1

Tag Silver twist.
Tail Some sprigs from the saddle-feathers of a golden pheasant.
Body Very rough pig's wool, a sort of orange brown at tail, merging into more and more brown, until it is dark bear's brown at the shoulder.

Mr Rowell's No. 1

Rib	Medium gold tinsel.
Hackle	(Body and shoulder) Coch-y-bonddu hackle with plenty of black at the butt.
Wings	The under wing is two slips of grey drake, and two of light dun turkey over.
Head	None. (See Dee flies, below.)
Hooks	7 or 8

No. 2

Very much the same, only the body is a trifle yellower at the tail. The tail is of tippet sprigs and the body is not so deep a brown up at the shoulder. The under wing is of peacock, not too bright, and the upper of dark dun turkey.

Hooks 7 or 8

No. 3

Tail and hackle, as in No. 1; body, bright medium brown throughout; wing, peacock, brownish at the butt.

Hooks 7 or 8

No. 4

Tag	Gold tinsel.
Tail	Black partridge or teal and some golden pheasant saddle feather.
Butt	Black ostrich herl.
Body	The lower half is yellow inclining to orange. The upper half dark medium blue pig's wool.
Rib	Silver tinsel.
Hackle	Coch-y-bonddu.
Shoulder	Blue jay.
Wings	A mixed wing. The under part of pintail, teal, and tippet (dyed red); over this a golden pheasant sword feather, slips of claret and orange swan, and a good deal of golden pheasant tail over all.
Head	None. (See Dee flies, below.)
Hook	5

I had a further note from Sir Herbert with respect to the Annan and Nith, from which I extract the following:

Captain Stewart tells me that he always uses the different varieties of dun and white tip turkey and brown mallard as dressed by Jamie Wright of Sprouston [see Tweed flies, p. 9], that prince of dressers for Scottish waters. Also the Butcher, and a fly dressed as follows:

Tag	Silver tinsel.
Tail	Topping and red Indian crow.
Body	Half lemon yellow then half black mohair or pig's wool, according to the size of the fly.
Hackle	Coch-y-bonddu.
Shoulder	Black hackle.
Wings	A mixed wing of mallard, teal, yellow, and lavender swan, and plenty of red macaw, with or without a small tippet under. A topping over all.
Head	Black ostrich herl.
Hooks	6–12

THE ABERDEENSHIRE DEE

There are many Dees in the kingdom, two noted ones in Scotland and one famous river in England and Wales. That which I here refer to is the chief one, or the Aberdeenshire Dee. It is almost a pattern river for the skilful salmon-fisher, but will not admit of being fished by a muff; in fact it is by no means an easy river to fish. The lower reaches are not good rising ground, as the salmon run through and rise badly while resting – the Aboyne water perhaps being the cream of the Dee. The casts are rapid rough streams and often heavy, but it is perhaps one of the clearest streams in Scotland. The flies used are peculiar, and the local ones are of little use on any other river in Scotland, save perhaps a small size of the Gled Wing, or the Tartan, which may be used for the Don. The flies are usually large, but slenderly dressed, being meant to catch the salmon's eye, I presume, in the deep rough water (which a small fly would not), and not to frighten him, which too gross an imposition perhaps might do. Some of the flies used, as the Eagle (local 'aigle') – I say, the 'aigle' is little more marvellous as a fly than the local dialect is a dialect; and if we might liken some flies to shrimps and prawns, and others to butterflies and dragonflies, the Eagle completely knocks all such possibilities on the head, as it is like nothing on, over, or under the earth or water that I know of. The Dee flies are dressed upon hooks specially made for them; these are very long in the shank, with the Limerick bend. The large class of flies run from about No. 2 in the given scale, down to No. 6, but with this condition: the shank of the hook which represents the No. 2 *size of bend* is just an inch longer for the Dee flies, while that of No. 6 is an inch and a half, the intermediate ones being of proportionate length. For smaller flies, Limerick hooks are used, even down to No. 7 or 8 hook.

The Gled Wing *Colour plate 3*
This fly, sometimes called the Red Wing, is perhaps the most useful of the local flies.

Tag Silver tinsel.
Tail Golden pheasant saddle.
Body One-third orange-yellow, and two-thirds claret, or light purple claret mohair, dressed very sparsely.
Rib Broadish silver tinsel laid on rather thinly and in long spirals.
Hackle Black heron's hackle of the largest size, or two, if one will not go far enough, dressed down to the yellow mohair; they must be of the longest fibre, the longer the better.
Shoulder Teal hackle, without which no Dee fly is thought complete.
Wings Two good slips of swallow-tailed gled (kite) of the longest fibre, or of red dun turkey of the like colour. Of course these feathers must be of thin substance and fine in the fibre, to give them play, and they are to be set apart – a rather nice operation to do neatly; the strips requiring to be carefully prepared first by tying in at the extreme butt.
Head There is no head, as it is thought to cause a ripple, while the sharp head of the regular Dee fly cuts the water with a smooth even gliding motion, opening and shutting its large fibres with a most lifelike appearance.
Hooks 2–6 (long shank). 7–8 smaller flies.

The Tartan *Colour plate 3*
This is a strange-looking fly, and is a rather troublesome fly to dress.

Tag Gold tinsel.
Tail Golden pheasant rump.
Body Half orange and half scarlet-red mohair laid on sparely.
Rib Broadish gold tinsel also spare.
Hackle First a stripped sandy-red cock's hackle (that is, only one side of it to be used, the other being stripped off), and on top of this, the large blue-grey hackle or feather from the heron's back and rump; the larger the better, they cannot be too large, as when the hackle is laid on the fibres are expected to extend from the very head to the farthest bend of the hook. It is an awkward feather to lay on, as are all heron's hackles, being very delicate. It should be tied in to commence from as low down as it can be conveniently tied, so as to leave enough for a good thick brush from the head. In winding on the hackle, if any of the red hackle fibres under it be wound in, they must be picked out afterwards with the needle and put in their proper position.
Shoulder A teal hackle, of course.
Wings Two strips of silver-grey mottled turkey (the small mottled feather); these feathers are not easy to get.
Head As before.
Hooks As before.

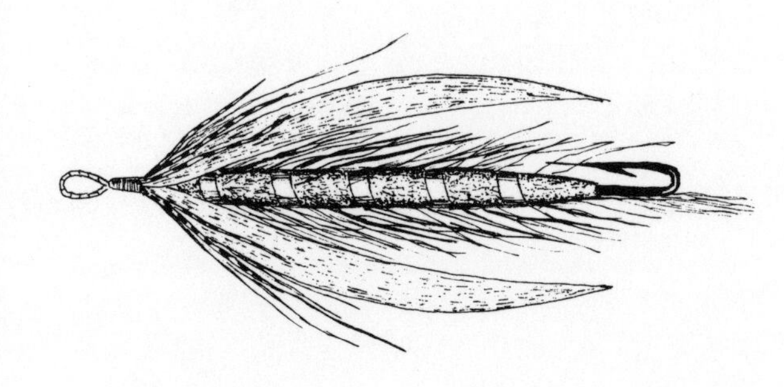

A Strip Wing Dee Fly: from above, showing the correct position of the wings

When this fly is finished, and before it is properly pressed down into shape, it looks like an enormous spider, or daddy longlegs; it certainly is a monstrosity, though, after all, not such a monstrosity as the following fly.

The Eagle *Colour plate 3*
There are two Eagles, the grey and the yellow. The yellow is simply the same feather as the grey, only dyed a bright canary yellow; indeed, I believe, in the evening, the 'yalley aigle' is the favourite, and is the more effective fly of the two. The tail, body etc. are precisely similar to those of the Gled Wing; a quantity of the down or fluffy part of the golden eagle's feather itself; on the shoulder is of course the invariable teal hackle. The wings are two broadish strips of silver-grey turkey, the large mottled or broad stripped and banded feather being selected.
The above are local flies, but a claret body and hackle, with mixed wing of long brown turkey, argus, and bustard feathers, with a gold pheasant sword feather in the midst, does well also; as does the black body and silver tinsel, with gallina shoulder and mixed wing. (Marabou makes a good substitute for eagle.)
Most of these flies are from Mr Brown's patterns, the well-known tackle-maker of Aberdeen, the inventor of the phantom minnow. He dresses them as few others can. Since the last list was made up Mr Brown writes me word that few changes of any note have taken place. He says:

> I do not know of any 'Standard Patterns', other than what you have. Everyone who can make a fly makes new patterns, but those who use the plain flies use the patterns you have in the book; but a great many fishermen are going into the gay flies, such as Jock Scott, Silver Doctor, Childers, Butcher, Popham etc., which you know very well. For my part I generally try what I have been generally successful with on former occasions, though I, like others, go in now and then for the gay patterns.
>
> *W. Brown*

THE DON

The Don enters the North Sea a very short distance from the Dee, but no two rivers can well be more dissimilar; the Dee running through the wildest moorland and mountain scenery, and having no trout in it worth notice, and the Don running through beautiful pastoral and well-tilled districts, looking more like a Hampshire than a Highland salmon stream, and containing perhaps as fine trout as any river in Scotland. Yet the salmon seem to like very similar flies; a small reduction in point of size being made. The Don flies are not so large as those for the Dee, though after the same fashion. Indeed, smallish Dee flies are fair size Don flies. As on the Dee, the Gled Wings and Tartans are standard flies on the Don, and are varied by using brown or grey mallard wings. Beyond these are the following patterns tied by Mr Brown of Aberdeen.

No. 1

Tag	Silver tinsel.
Tail	A few fibres of golden pheasant's rump and a small tuft of yellow crewel.
Butt	Black ostrich herl.
Body	Black pig's wool.
Rib	Silver twist.
Hackle	Black.
Shoulder	Blue jay.
Wings	Gled (swallow-tailed kite) or dun turkey strips.
Head	None. (See Dee flies p. 12)
Hooks	7–10

No. 2

Tag	Silver tinsel.
Tail	Golden pheasant's rump and a small tuft of yellow crewel (as before).
Butt	Black ostrich herl.
Body	About two-fifths dark red, and three-fifths dark blue pig's wool.
Rib	None.
Hackle	None.
Shoulder	Light blue with a short grouse hackle over.

Wings	Strips of the red dun turkey feather speckled with black.
Head	None.
Hooks	7–10

No. 3

Tag	Gold tinsel.
Tail	A tuft of orange crewel.
Body	Two-thirds orange and one-third black pig's wool.
Rib	Narrow gold tinsel.
Hackle	Starting half way along body on to shoulder, a large coch-y-bonddu hackle with well marked centre.
Wings	Strips of grey mallard with brownish points.
Head	None.
Hooks	9–11

No. 4

Tail	A few golden pheasant rump fibres.
Body	Half yellow and half medium red pig's wool.
Rib	Gold twist.
Hackle	Half way along body to shoulder, a small black heron's hackle just long enough in the fibre to cover the point of the barb.
Wings	Grey mallard with brownish points (as before).
Head	Black.
Hooks	9–11

No. 5

Tail	A small topping.
Body	Purple claret pig's wool.
Rib	Silver twist.
Shoulder	(No body hackle.) Black heron dressed spare, and longer in the fibre than the bend of the hook.
Wings	Two strips of gled or red turkey.
Head	None.
Hooks	9–11

No. 6

Tag	Gold tinsel.
Tail	A small topping.
Body	Brown-orange mohair.
Rib	Gold tinsel.
Shoulder	(No body hackle.) Blue heron's hackle, the fibres extending to about the bend of the hook.
Wings	Two strips of bright speckled grey turkey.
Head	None.
Hooks	9–11

Mr Brown's No. 4

THE DEVERON

Nos. 3, 4, 5, and 6 of the Don flies last described are standard patterns for the Deveron. Patterns from Mr Brown.

THE NESS

The Ness is a large and heavy river issuing from a very large water, Loch Ness, which is fed by several good salmon streams, of which the Garry is perhaps the most noteworthy. The Garry is an excellent early spring river, whereas the Ness, through which all the Garry fish run, is but an indifferent one. The Ness is a fair summer river, and also gives plenty of grilse and large sea-trout to the rod; later on the salmon run to the largest size. The streams and pools on the Ness are remarkably fine and bold. The casts are mostly fished from a boat, though in places they can be fished from the shore.

For so large a river as the Ness, the flies used are very small. One of the best killers which I found to answer on the Ness was an old Thurso pattern which I obtained from Mr Dunbar years ago. I had three of them which had lain in my book for years without being used; but if you keep a fly long enough it is sure to come in useful at last. Johnny Macdonald 'joost liked the look o' 'em', and I 'joost' took Johnny's 'adveece', and I did well with them when I distinctly failed with other flies. They had been dressed small, I conclude, for very early and late patterns, if they were meant for the Thurso.

No. 1

Tag	Silver tinsel and orange floss.
Tail	A topping and tippet sprigs.
Butt	Pale blue ostrich herl.
Body	Two turns of blue-green floss; yellowish olive-green pig's wool, with a bit of orange at the shoulder.
Rib	Silver tinsel.
Shoulder	(No body hackle.) Bright claret hackle.
Wings	A tippet and saddle feather, golden pheasant tail, and a good bit of wood-duck on either side.
Head	Black.
Hooks	6–11

No. 2

Tag	Silver tinsel and lemon floss.
Tail	One topping.
Body	One third yellow, the rest dark red (almost claret) pig's wool.
Rib	Silver tinsel.
Shoulder	(No body hackle.) Medium blue mohair tied on in locks for a hackle with a grouse hackle over it.
Wings	A small tippet feather. Over this, strips of bustard, peacock, pintail, and dark orange-yellow swan.
Head	Black.
Hooks	6–11

No. 3

This is also a capital fly on the Ness or anywhere else; it is a nice warm fly and a favourite of mine.

Tag	Gold tinsel and yellow floss.
Tail	A topping.
Body	Orange-yellow, merging into distinct orange, and that again into a red-brown or burnt sienna at the shoulder, some of it picked out at the breast; each of pig's wool.
Rib	None.
Hackle	None.
Shoulder	A grouse hackle.
Wings	Sprigs of pintail, bustard, peacock, and tippet, and one topping over all.
Head	Black.
Hooks	6–11

No. 4

Tag	Silver tinsel and blue floss.
Tail	A topping.
Butt	Black ostrich herl.
Body	Three turns of gold-coloured floss; the rest bright yellow pig's wool.
Rib	Silver tinsel.
Hackle	Orange-yellow hackle over the wool only.
Shoulder	A light purple claret hackle.
Wings	A mixed wing of golden pheasant tail, pintail, gallina fibres; red, yellow, and orange swan fibres.
Cheeks	Kingfisher.
Horns	Blue macaw.
Head	Black.
Hooks	6–11

No. 5

This is also a good general fly; the body is somewhat like one of the Conon bodies (see p. 19). The same with pea-green pig's wool and hackle makes a good change.

Tail	A topping.
Body	Half yellow and half lightish medium blue pig's wool.
Rib	Silver twist.
Hackle	Medium blue.

Shoulder Grouse hackle.
Wings One tippet feather and strips of golden pheasant tail, bustard and pintail over it.
Horns A few strips of golden pheasant sword feather.
Head Black.
Hooks 6–11

No. 6
Tag Silver tinsel, and one turn of ruby floss.
Tail One topping.
Body Orange merging to brown, and that into blue pig's wool, dressed roughish.
Shoulder (No body hackle.) Darkish medium blue.
Wings A tippet feather and slips of brown mallard and pintail over it; two short pea-green parrot feathers over the butts of these feathers.
Horns Blue macaw.
Head Black.
Hooks 6–11

No. 7
This is also a capital fly for the Shin (see p. 25).
Tag Silver tinsel and orange floss.
Tail None.
Butt Black ostrich herl.
Body Three turns of gold-coloured floss, the rest black mohair.
Rib Silver tinsel.
Hackle Black.
Shoulder Blue jay.
Wings Slices of yellow and orange swan, brown, and grey mallard and golden pheasant tail, a few sprigs of tippet, and a topping over all.
Cheeks Kingfisher.
Horns Blue macaw.
Head Black.
Hooks 6–11

The Denison *Colour plate 4*
This fly is said to kill well at all times on the Ness, and as the late Speaker's brother, who is the godfather to it, is a very successful fisherman there, we may conclude that the information is pretty accurate.
Tag One turn of silver twist, one of claret, and one of yellow floss.
Tail One topping and a slip of wood-duck.
Butt Black ostrich herl.
Body One half silver thread, the other half light blue floss.
Rib Silver twist.
Hackle Light blue over the floss only.
Shoulder Blue jay.
(So far the fly is a compromise between the two Doctors. The wing, however, is peculiar, having a greasy look from the two golden pheasant rump feathers in it.)
Wings Two tippet feathers with a jungle-cock on either side as long as the hook; over these two golden pheasant rump feathers (same size as the tippet); one topping over all.
Horns Blue macaw.
Head Black.
Hooks 6–11
It is a showy fly, but I would banish the rump feathers and use a jungle-cock instead. I think it would be quite as attractive and would lose that greasy look which I do not admire.

The Highlander
I have included this fly in the list of Ness flies, though I think it is better for the Carron and some Ross'shire rivers than the Ness. It is the best fly you can use on the Carron.
Tag Silver twist and gold floss.
Tail A topping.
Butt Black ostrich herl.
Body For a small fly, gold-coloured floss nearly half way up the body, above this dirty olive-green mohair. For a large fly, a few turns of gold-coloured floss, then yellow pig's wool followed by dirty olive-green mohair as before.
Rib Silver tinsel.
Hackle Pea-green hackle from tail to head.
Shoulder Blue jay.

Wings Sprigs of tippet, golden pheasant tail and mallard with pintail over. Double jungle-cock on either side, and a topping over all.
Head Black.
Hooks 6–11

The two Doctors and the Popham are often used with advantage, and the Claret and the Highlander may be found useful at times.
The Ness flies are usually small, not larger than grilse flies, and even in a heavy water a very moderate-sized fly is sufficient. They run from 6 or 7 to 10 or 11.

THE GARRY OF LOCH NESS

This is a spring river and requires large flies – Nos. 3 and 4. These three flies are sent to me by Mr Snowie, of Inverness, who is the best authority for flies upon the rivers in Inverness, Nairn, Elgin, Ross, Sutherland, and Caithness.

No. 1
Tag Silver tinsel and lemon floss.
Tail A topping and some black partridge.
Butt Black ostrich herl.
Body Three or four turns of orange floss, dark orange pig's wool (almost red) for one-third, then a lighter and browner orange for the rest of the body, dressed roughish and picked out.
Rib Broad silver tinsel and gold twist.
Hackle Bright orange.
Shoulder Light blue with gallina over it.
Wings Under wing, a tippet, strips of bustard, peacock, and golden pheasant tail. Over wing, a sword feather; jungle-cock on either side, and topping over all.
Horns Blue macaw.
Head Black.
Hooks 3 and 4

No. 2
Tag Gold tinsel and mulberry, and gold-coloured floss.
Tail A topping and some sprigs of tippet and wood-duck.
Butt Black ostrich herl.
Body Three or four turns of gold-coloured floss silk; the remainder is a mixture of medium green and yellow pig's wool, the green predominating.
Rib Broad silver tinsel and gold twist side by side.
Hackle Black.
Shoulder Gallina (pretty thick).
Wings Under wing, a tippet feather and a sword feather; over wing, strips of orange, yellow, and dark claret-red swan, strips of golden pheasant tail, brown mallard and bustard; teal on either side and a topping over all.
Horns Blue macaw.
Head Black.
Hooks 3 and 4

No. 3
Tag Silver tinsel and gold-coloured floss.
Tail A topping.
Butt Black ostrich herl.
Body One-third gold-coloured floss, the rest darkish red pig's wool.
Rib Silver tinsel.
Hackle Black.
Shoulder Blue jay.
Wings A slice or two of golden pheasant tippet, two or three slices of orange swan, strips of grey mallard and golden pheasant tail, with double jungle-cock on either side.
Horns Blue macaw.
Head Black.
Hooks 3 and 4

The Snow Fly *Colour plate 4*
This is another capital fly for the Garry in early spring. It is almost, if not quite, impervious. It kills well also on the Helmsdale.

Tag Silver tinsel.
Tail Ibis, wood-duck, and a small topping.
Butt A turn or two of black wool.
Body The body is in four joints, and is composed of stout silver twist. At every joint a wad of pig's wool is tied in and picked out; this at the first joint is light blue, at the second medium claret, at the third orange, and the head of the fourth (on the shoulder) is yellow, picked out to answer for a hackle. Over this is a short orange hackle, the main fibre of which is well covered by the butt of the wings.
Wings Slices of golden pheasant tail, bustard, turkey, and sprigs of green, pink, and orange swan, and dark turkey dyed red.
Head Blue wool.
Hooks 3 and 4

THE CONON

The Conon is a large river which has some capital tributaries, the best of which is perhaps the Blackwater, which for its length is usually very well stocked with fish. The upper parts of the Conon are very pretty and tempting, containing fine streams and good pools, but the lower reaches are heavy and dull. The fish for the most part run through them without resting long, and while they do rest rise but indifferently.
Here are three flies for the Conon, all of which are first-rate general flies and will kill anywhere.

No. 1
Tag Two turns of silver tinsel.
Tail A topping and some sprigs of tippet.
Body One turn of bright orange brown, continued with yellow half-way up, and the remaining half with medium (inclining to light) blue pig's wool, dressed rough and well picked out.
Rib Broadish silver tinsel.
Shoulder (No body hackle.) A pretty thick black hackle.
Wings Bright mottled peacock with a shortish jungle-cock on either side, rather better than half the length of the wing.
Head Black.
Hooks 5–8

No. 2
Tag Two turns of silver tinsel.
Tail A topping and some sprigs of tippet.
Body One turn of bright orange brown, continuing with yellow half-way up, and the remaining half of black pig's wool.
Rib Broadish silver tinsel.
Hackle A black hackle over the black wool, finishing on the shoulder.
Wings One tippet feather with bright peacock over it. Short jungle-cock on either side.
Head Black.
Hooks 5–8

No. 3
Tag Two turns of silver tinsel.
Tail A topping and some sprigs of tippet.
Body Olive yellow changing into dirty orange, and that again into purple claret at the shoulder, each of pig's wool.
Rib Silver tinsel.
Hackle Black hackle from tail to head, serving also as a shoulder hackle.
Wings Peacock.
Head Black.
Hooks 5–8

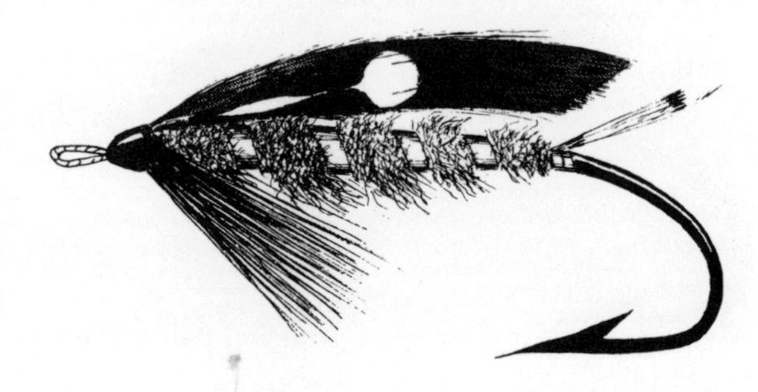

No. 1 for the Conon

THE LOCHY

I now give four flies for the Lochy. The Lochy flies should be dressed smaller even than those for the Ness, not much above sea-trout size. These patterns are from Mr Farlow of 191, The Strand.

No. 1

Tag	Silver twist.
Tail	A topping and three or four sprigs of red parrot.
Body	Two turns of yellow, two of red, and the rest of black crewel.
Rib	Gold tinsel.
Shoulder	(No body hackle.) Black hackle with a blue jay over it.
Wings	Under wing, a tippet feather with slips of brown mallard over. Over wing, mixed wood-duck and gallina.
Horns	Blue macaw.
Head	Black.
Hooks	7–11

No. 2

Tag	Silver twist and orange floss.
Tail	One topping with a few mixed sprigs of tippet and wood-duck.
Butt	Black peacock herl.
Body	Pale blue floss.
Rib	Fine silver thread, doubled.
Hackle	Lightish red claret from butt to head.
Shoulder	Two turns of blue jay.
Wings	Golden pheasant tail and tippet sprigs, with mixed lightish mallard and gallina over.
Head	Black.
Hooks	7–11

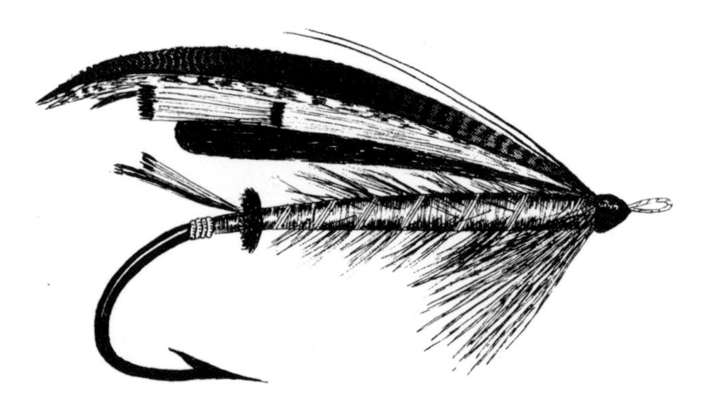

Mr Farlow's No. 3

No. 3

Tag	Silver twist and ruby floss.
Tail	Sprigs of tippet and black partridge.
Butt	Black ostrich herl.
Body	Two turns of blue, two of ruby, the rest of a dirty orange, or olive-yellow floss.
Rib	Gold thread doubled.
Hackle	Olive hackle from ruby floss to head.
Shoulder	Grouse hackle (from the rump of the bird).
Wings	A strip of dark (almost black) turkey, with a tippet over, sprigs of tippet, bustard, bright red and yellow stained gallina over that, and mallard above all.
Horns	Blue macaw.
Head	Black.
Hooks	7–11

No. 4

Tag	Silver tinsel and orange floss.
Tail	A yellow toucan feather or a topping.
Body	Dark mulberry floss.
Rib	Gold tinsel.
Hackle	Brown claret. (I should call it 'fiery brown'.)
Shoulder	A grouse hackle.
Wings	A strip of dark (almost black) turkey, with a tippet over, sprigs of tippet, bustard, bright red and yellow gallina over that, and mallard above all. (Same as No. 3.)
Head	Black.
Hooks	7–11

THE THURSO

The Thurso is one of the best early spring rivers in Scotland and seldom fails in yielding sport. It is not a large river, but is fed by several small lakes. It is extremely prolific, but rather a dull dead stream, is perfectly open, devoid of high banks, and very easy to fish. For all these reasons it is a capital river to enter a green hand on, or for those who are not equal to much fatigue, or to whom wading is tabooed. The flies for it should be dressed on good-sized hooks; the middle sizes, not so large as Dee and Tay hooks, nor so small as Ness flies, being preferable. These flies are also from Farlow's; the fish having undergone a complete change in their tastes since I was here; for when I was there they preferred a sober coloured fly, but of late years they prefer more showy ones. Mr Dunbar, the lessee of the river, to whom I wrote lately, tells me that there is no change in the bill of fare; the same flies are used now as were used half-a-dozen years ago.

The Dhoon Fly *Colour plate 4*
This was originally a Mahseer fly used in the Himalayas. How it came to be adopted here I cannot say, but it kills on one or two other rivers, particularly in spring on the Welsh Wye, where it is called the Canary.

Tag Gold tinsel and ruby floss.
Tail A topping.
Butt Black ostrich herl.
Body In four joints of bright yellow floss; at every joint a large wad of yellow wool is tied in for a hackle and left long and bushy; in the two lower joints it is plain yellow wool, the upper two joints have at them bright orange-yellow pig's wool, very long and bushy.
Rib Gold twist.
Shoulder (No body hackle.) A yellow hackle with an orange hackle over it.
Wings Two big strips of swan feather dyed bright orange.
Cheeks Two good long kingfisher or chatterer feathers.
Head Black.
Hooks 4–10

The Duke of Sutherland
Tag Silver twist and gold-coloured floss.
Tail A topping, some tippet sprigs with green and red parrot.
Butt Black ostrich herl.
Body Two turns of burnt sienna floss, two turns of bright medium green floss (by medium I mean that it is neither a decidedly yellow nor a decidedly blue-green, but strictly medium), the rest of pig's wool of the same colour.
Rib Gold twist and silver tinsel.
Hackle Bright medium green to match the pig's wool.
Shoulder Orange-yellow hackle.
Wings Under wing, two tippet feathers. Over wing, strips of bustard and golden pheasant tail; over them, sprigs of yellow-green swan, and a topping over all.
Cheeks Himalaya pheasant back feather (that with the white spots on it).
Horns Blue macaw.
Head Black.
Hooks 4–10

Sir Francis Sykes
Tag Silver twist and blue floss.
Tail A topping with sprigs of teal and blue macaw.
Body Dark cinnamon-brown floss.
Rib Silver twist, doubled.
Hackle Dark cinnamon-brown, over half the body and at shoulder.
Wings A mixed wing of golden pheasant tail, tippet, bustard, wood-duck, blue, red, yellow and green swan sprigs.
Head Red.
Hooks 4–10

The Priest
This is a good general fly, killing well in many parts of Ireland too.
Tag Gold twist and dark blue floss.
Tail A topping and pale red ibis or flamingo.
Butt Black ostrich herl.

Body	Three turns of orange floss, the rest dirty olive-brown mohair.
Rib	Gold tinsel and silver twist side by side.
Hackle	Golden olive.
Shoulder	A medium blue hackle.
Wings	Dark turkey, or cock-pheasant tail, over this fibres of bustard, and bright florican bustard, brown mallard and a plentiful admixture of green swan sprigs.
Head	Red.
Hooks	4–10

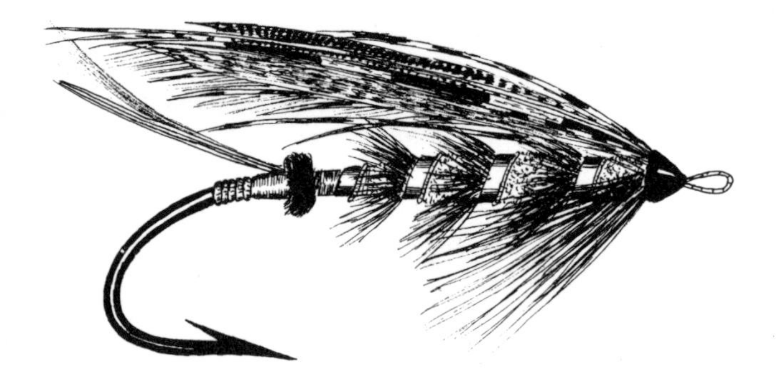

The Priest

Switching Sandy

The body and hackle of this fly are so like the Highlander, that it will be found to kill on the Ness, the Carron, the Blackwater, the Garry, and many other Ross and Sutherlandshire rivers: on many of these rivers, greens are in favour.

Tag	Silver tinsel and light orange-red floss.
Tail	A topping and tippet sprigs.
Butt	Black ostrich herl.
Body	Three turns of dark blue floss, two of yellow-green floss, the rest of blue-green wool.
Rib	Gold tinsel.
Hackle	Light yellow-green.
Shoulder	A blue-green hackle slightly darker than the body hackle.
Wings	Natural golden pheasant tail, and another dyed pinkish, shreds of brown mallard, wood-duck and florican bustard, blue and yellow-green swan sprigs.
Head	Black.
Hooks	4–10

Other favourite flies for the Thurso are the Black and Teal, the Britannia, the Childers, the Namsen, the Butcher and the Major. Sizes from 4 to 10.

THE LAXFORD

These patterns for the Laxford are also from Farlow's. The first fly has no name, and as that is a very inconvenient hiatus, particularly as it would be a capital general fly, I call it:

The Laxford

Tag	Gold twist.
Tail	One topping.
Body	Gold-coloured floss silk.
Rib	Silver tinsel and gold twist.
Hackle	Bright yellow.
Shoulder	A darkish blue hackle.
Wings	A lump of peacock, over it sprigs of bustard and florican bustard, and a topping over all.
Head	Black.
Hooks	9 and 10

The Lascelles

Tag	Silver twist and lemon-yellow floss.
Tail	A topping and some blue macaw sprigs.
Butt	Black ostrich herl.
Body	Half lemon-yellow floss, and half pig's wool of the same colour.
Rib	Silver twist with black silk beside it, as in the Colonel.
Hackle	Claretty brown (this, as in the case of No. 4 in the Lochy list, is what I consider fiery brown).
Shoulder	Speckled gallina.

Wings	A golden pheasant rump and a saddle feather, sprigs of golden pheasant tail, and florican bustard, yellow and blue swan sprigs, with a few fibres of golden pheasant sword feather, over all a good slice of gallina.
Head	Black.
Hooks	9 and 10

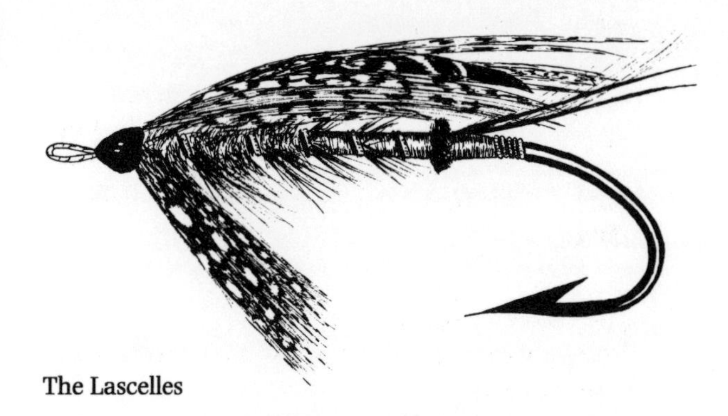

The Lascelles

THE AWE AND THE ORCHY

The same flies are used on both these rivers. I wrote asking a friend to obtain patterns for me if possible, and he got them for me from Colonel Campbell of Skipness, whose reputation as a sportsman is only second to his fame as an author; for few, if any, modern books of sporting adventure can compare in point of general interest and sportsmanlike handling with the *Old Forest Ranger* and *My Indian Journal*, both of which are the productions of Colonel Campbell's pen. He sends four flies.

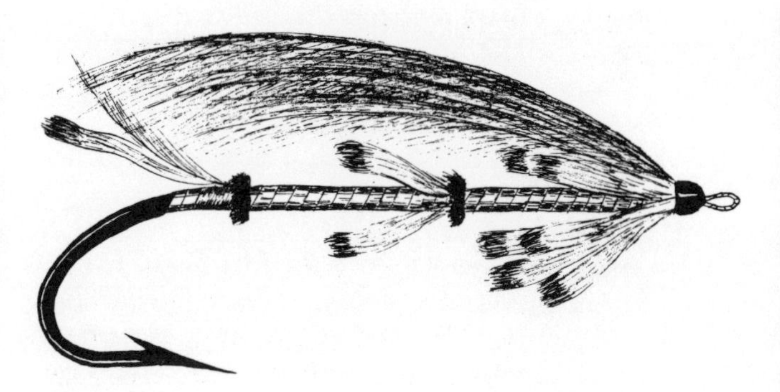

The Canary

The Canary

This fly is more often called the Goldfinch, and I mention the fact as another fly has already been saddled with the same appellation. I have given one Goldfinch dressing (see p. 6), but as there is some variety in this, I give the Colonel's as well.

Tag	Gold tinsel and gold-coloured floss.
Tail	A topping and a short yellow toucan feather.
Butt	Black ostrich herl.
Body	Gold tinsel in two joints, divided by two turns of black ostrich herl, with short yellow toucan feathers tied in at the joints for hackles, as in the fashion of the Popham. Those at the breast should increase a size larger of course.
Wings	Five or six toppings.
Horns	Blue macaw.
Head	Black.
Hooks	6–9

Of this the Colonel says: 'Good either for Awe or Orchy, particularly when the water is low.'

The Indian Crow

The Colonel says of this fly: 'So called from the feathers of the Indian crow in the body. I tried this fly for the first time about five years ago, and I have killed with it and the Butcher, more and larger fish than with any other; a deadly fly in any river on which I have tried it.'

This fly is a slight variation of the Popham.

Tag	Gold twist.
Tail	A topping.
Butt	Black ostrich herl. (Also between each body joint.)
Body	In three joints, the lower joint being orange-yellow floss, the next two light blue, each joint is separated by a few turns of black ostrich herl which are tied in over the small red feathers from the breast of an Indian crow.

Rib Silver thread.
Shoulder Light blue hackle.
Wings Mixed fibres of golden pheasant tail, tippet, bustard, teal, and blue, yellow, and claret-dyed swan; a topping over all.
Head Black.
Hooks 6–9

The Colonel's Butcher

No two tyers dress the Butcher alike – this is the Colonel's pattern.

Tag Gold twist and orange floss.
Tail One topping.
Butt Black ostrich herl.
Body Red, medium blue, red, and medium blue pig's wool in equal portions.
Rib Broad silver tinsel.
Hackle Brown olive with a turn of jay at the breast.
Shoulder Gallina.
Wings Mixed of tippet and golden pheasant tail, a good deal of bustard, a little gallina, blue, red and yellow swan, a topping over all, and a pair of jungle-cock at the sides.
Head Black.
Hooks 4–10

The Colonel says: 'Good either on the Awe or the Orchy'; and he adds, 'the water being very clear both in the Awe and Orchy, single gut must always be used.'

Mr Macnicol's No. 3

Colonel Campbell has also sent another fly which is almost identical with No. 1 in the Conon patterns (see p. 19). The only difference I can discern is that the turn of orange-brown pig's wool which commences the tail end of the fly is transferred to the shoulder, and the colours run yellow, blue, and orange. The jungle-cock is also wanting. The Colonel says of this fly, this is 'the old legitimate Orchy and Awe fly, and is considered a "great medicine" by the natives, who ignore all others.' Hook size 8.

I have also half-a-dozen patterns for the Awe from Malcolm Macnicol, of Dalmally, who is *the* tyer of flies for all that part of the country. Malcolm is a first-rate hand either with rod and gaff or dubbing and feather. Here are his patterns. They are all sober flies, in black and grey coats.

No. 1

Tag Silver thread and one turn of orange floss.
Tail A small topping.
Body Black mohair.
Rib Medium silver tinsel.
Hackle Black, to shoulder.
Wings Either strips of silver-grey mottled turkey, or a bit of good bright peacock.
Head Black.
Hooks 7 and 8

No. 2

Tag Silver thread and one turn of orange floss.
Tail A small topping.
Body One turn of light yellow mohair, the rest of black mohair.
Rib Medium silver tinsel.
Hackle Black, to shoulder.
Wings Strips of bluish-black heron's wing.
Head Black.
Hooks 7 and 8

A similar fly to No. 1.

No. 3

Tag Three or four turns of fine gold twist.
Tail A good-sized Indian crow feather.

Butt A turn of scarlet crewel.
Body A darkish shade of blue mohair.
Rib Silver tinsel.
Hackle A darkish shade of blue to match the body.
Shoulder A brown grouse, partridge, or bustard hackle.
Wings Strips of silver-grey mottled turkey or peacock.
Head Black.
Hooks 7 and 8

No. 4
Tag Silver thread and blue floss.
Tail Tippet and some fibres from a claret hackle.
Butt Black ostrich herl.
Body Two turns of yellow pig's wool, the rest of darkish pea-green floss.
Rib Silver tinsel.
Hackle Lightish yellow-green.
Shoulder Blue jay.
Wings Speckled brown turkey, grey towards the tips.
Head Black.
Hooks 7 and 8

No. 5
Tag Silver thread.
Tail A bit of orange mohair and teal.
Body Two turns of medium pea-green floss, and the rest of bright medium blue mohair, a few fibres of light claret mohair being thrown in at the shoulder.
Rib Silver tinsel.
Hackle Light claret, to shoulder.
Wings Slips of black heron.
Head Black.
Hooks 7 and 8

No. 6
Tag Silver thread.
Tail A good-sized Indian crow feather.
Body Two turns of yellow pig's wool, the rest darkish blue mohair, with a pinch of fiery red pig's wool thrown in at the shoulder.
Rib Silver tinsel.
Hackle Black, to shoulder.
Wings Silver-grey mottled turkey or peacock.
Head Black.
Hooks 7 and 8

THE SHIN

This is a very fine river, often showing excellent sport. In the spring the salmon are seldom found above the falls (Falls of Shin), but as the summer gets on the higher reaches become better stocked. This river was for many years in the hands of my poor old friend Andrew Young, whose name is so well known in the history of the salmon. Since his death it has been let out in rods, or to private hands.
The following three patterns are from Mr Snowie.

No. 1
Tag Gold tinsel and orange floss.
Tail One topping.
Butt Black ostrich herl.
Body Two or three turns of gold-coloured floss, then half yellow and half bright claret-red pig's wool.
Rib None.
Hackle Black.
Shoulder Light claret.
Wings Under wing, a tippet. Over wing, strips of peacock, golden pheasant tail, mallard, peacock stained pale yellow; a topping over all.
Horns Blue macaw.
Hooks 6–10 to suit the water.

No. 2
Tag Silver tinsel and gold floss.
Tail A topping.
Butt Black ostrich herl.

Body One-third gold floss, the rest light olive-green mohair.
Rib Silver tinsel.
Hackle Black.
Shoulder Blue jay.
Wings Two short golden pheasant saddle feathers, over this strips of golden pheasant tail and common hen pheasant tail. On either side a good slice of bustard and pintail with a few fibres of tippet; one topping over all.
Cheeks Kingfisher.
Horns Blue macaw.
Head Black.
Hooks 6–10

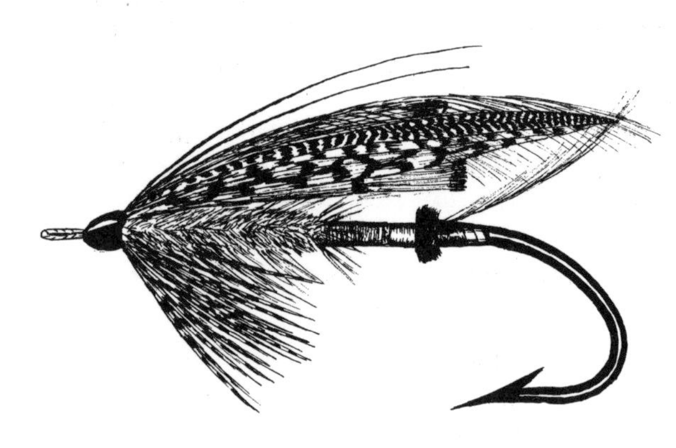

Mr Snowie's No. 3

Mr Farlow's No. 1

No. 3
Tag Silver tinsel and mulberry floss.
Tail A topping.
Butt Black ostrich herl.
Body Two turns of gold floss; one-third yellow, the rest very dark olive pig's wool.
Rib None.
Hackle Black.
Shoulder Blue jay.
Wings Under wing, a tippet feather. Over wing, golden pheasant tail, pintail, mallard, a golden pheasant rump feather, and a topping over all.
Horns Blue macaw.
Head Black.
Hooks 6–10

THE OYKEL

The following three patterns are from Farlow's.

No. 1
Tag Silver twist and pale yellow floss.
Tail A topping and kingfisher.
Body Black floss.
Rib Silver twist, bright red floss, and silver tinsel (the floss in the middle), all wound on together in equal breadth to the black floss.
Hackle A wisp of mohair at the breast; over this a few strands of gallina and blue jay, about one turn of each, finishing on the shoulder with black heron's hackle over all. The heron's hackle should not be too thick and long enough to reach the bend of the hook.
Shoulder See above.
Wings Golden pheasant tail and tippet fibres, over it some teal, bustard, and gallina.
Horns Yellow macaw.
Head Orange-yellow crewel.
Hooks 6–8

No. 2

Tag	Gold twist and orange-yellow floss.
Tail	A topping.
Body	Copper red floss.
Rib	Medium silver tinsel.
Hackle	Medium olive.
Shoulder	Bustard hackle.
Wings	Florican bustard and gallina, with dirty red and yellow swan fibres, and brown mallard over.
Horns	Blue macaw.
Head	Black.
Hooks	6–8

No. 3

Tag	Gold twist and burnt sienna floss.
Tail	Tippet and gallina fibres.
Butt	Black ostrich herl.
Body	One quarter medium orange floss, the rest of black floss.
Rib	Silver tinsel.
Hackle	Greenish olive.
Shoulder	One turn of yellowish olive hackle.
Wings	Orange-yellow and dirty red swan fibres, with a few blue macaw, slips of bustard, and a thin slice of silver mottled turkey or peacock in the middle.
Horns	Blue macaw.
Head	Black.
Hooks	6–8

THE BRORA

The following patterns are from Mr Snowie.

No. 1

Tag	Silver twist and gold-coloured floss.
Tail	A topping.
Body	Two turns of gold-coloured floss, the rest medium brown mohair.
Rib	Silver tinsel.
Shoulder	(No body hackle.) Longish-fibred black hackle.
Wings	A strip of peacock stained yellow, golden pheasant tail, sprigs of tippet, and slips of teal on either side; a topping over all.
Head	Black.
Hooks	6–10

No. 2

Tag	Silver tinsel and orange floss.
Tail	A topping.
Butt	Black ostrich herl.
Body	Half orange floss and half black mohair.
Rib	None.
Shoulder	(No body hackle.) Gallina.
Wings	Under wing, a bit of longish tippet. Over wing, orange-yellow, and claret strips of swan, golden pheasant tail, mallard, pintail, and a topping over all.
Cheeks	Short jungle-cock.
Horns	Blue macaw.
Head	Black.
Hooks	6–10

The John Scott

This is a very tasty-looking fly, being decorated with what is called in Ireland a mane. (See Owenmore fly, p. 49.)

Tag	Silver tinsel and gold-coloured floss.
Tail	A topping.
Butt	Blue ostrich herl.
Body	Half gold-coloured floss and half medium blue floss.
Rib	Silver tinsel.

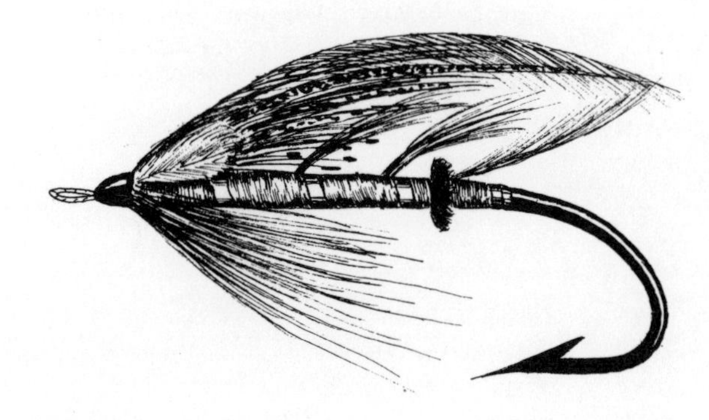

The John Scott

Mane	The mane is composed of locks of yellow-orange, purple claret, and medium blue mohair which flow from the back of the body above each turn of the rib.
Shoulder	A medium blue hackle, longish in the fibre.
Wings	Fibres of tippet, strips of black partridge and bustard on either side; a topping over all (the mane very much supplies the wing).
Cheeks	Kingfisher.
Head	Black.
Hooks	6–10

The Butcher, Popham, and Childers are also capital flies on the Brora.

THE HELMSDALE

This is a small river, rather dependent on rain, though it often yields good sport in the spring. The following patterns are from Mr Snowie.

No. 1

Tag	Silver twist and orange floss.
Tail	A topping.
Butt	Black ostrich herl.
Body	Three turns of orange floss, the rest of medium brown pig's wool.
Rib	Silver tinsel.
Hackle	A small black hackle.
Shoulder	A grouse hackle.
Wings	A slice of tippet, and strips of bustard, pintail, golden pheasant tail, gallina, and yellow swan; a topping over all.
Horns	Blue macaw.
Head	Black.
Hooks	7–10

No. 2

Tag	Silver twist.
Tail	A topping.
Butt	Black ostrich herl.
Body	One-third gold-coloured floss, the rest pea-green pig's wool.
Rib	Silver twist.
Shoulder	(No body hackle.) A grouse hackle tied in thickish.
Wings	A bit of tippet, strips of golden pheasant tail, teal, and plenty of orange swan sprigs; a topping over all.
Cheeks	Short jungle-cock.
Head	Black.
Hooks	7–10

No. 3

Tag	Silver tinsel and orange floss.
Tail	A topping.
Butt	Blue ostrich herl.
Body	Three turns of ruby floss, then olive and medium blue mohair in equal portions – roughish and picked out.
Rib	Silver twist.
Shoulder	(No body hackle.) A grouse hackle.
Wings	A bit of tippet, strips of gallina (the round spotted), golden pheasant tail, teal, and orange swan sprigs; a topping over all.
Cheeks	Short jungle-cock.
Head	Black.
Hooks	7–10

Add to these the Butcher, Childers, and the Snow Fly, noted above.

THE BEAULY

The Beauly is a fine river and belongs chiefly to Lord Lovat. The weir is a hard one to get up, and in the weir pool great numbers of fish are often congregated. Here, some years since, the Master of Lovat had in three days perhaps the most extraordinary sport ever known in Great Britain.
The following patterns are from Mr Snowie.

No. 1

Tag	Silver twist and gold-coloured floss.
Tail	A topping.
Butt	Black ostrich herl.

Body Two turns of gold floss, then half yellow and half black mohair.
Rib None.
Hackle Black over the black mohair only.
Shoulder Darkish blue (sparely), with blue jay over it.
Wings Two strips of tippet, golden pheasant tail, brown mallard, gallina, and yellow, red and orange swan sprigs; a topping over all.
Horns Blue macaw.
Hooks 5 and 6 for spring, 7 and 8 for summer.

No. 2
Tail A topping and mallard. (No tag or butt.)
Body Medium blue floss.
Rib Gold tinsel.
Hackle Medium blue to match the body.
Shoulder Gallina hackle with blue jay over it.
Wings Strips of dark and light turkey, some peacock herls, and a topping over all.
Hooks 5 and 6 for spring, 7 and 8 for summer.

The Beauly Snow Fly *Colour plate 5*
There is a singular fly used on the Beauly which is *there* termed the Snow Fly, and as long as there is any snow water in the river that fly kills well; far better indeed than any other. It is dressed on a big long-shanked round-bend hook like the Tay flies.
Tag No tag or tail.
Body Lightish blue pig's wool dressed sparely.
Rib Silver tinsel and gold twist.
Hackle A black heron's hackle (as long in the fibre or longer than the hook) starting about half-way up the body, and ending on the shoulder.
Wings A large bunch of bronze-coloured peacock herl.
A ruff of bright orange mohair is tied hackle-wise at the shoulder covering the butts of the wing and hackle fibres, which gives a brilliant and unusual look to the fly.
Head Black.
Hooks 1–4 long-shank, round-bend.

THE FINDHORN

The Findhorn is a very fine and lovely river, and the pools and streams perfection. At one time there was no river in Scotland that gave such sport to the rod, but the nets near the mouth, and incessant nettings of the lower pools, thin the fish and injure the sport greatly.
It can be fished from the shore but some of the casts require deepish wading. It is a long river with mountainous sources, and heavy rains may be going on back in the mountains, which the angler has no idea of, and the river will sometimes come down suddenly with a bore or a wave six feet high. The banks are high and rocky, and often inaccessible, and woe be to the angler if he is caught between them. The late Sir A. P. Gordon Cumming showed me one spot where he had had a very narrow escape. He had walked across a part of the river bed over which a little stream ran not higher than his ankles, to cast about 100 yards up the river. He was fishing the cast, when suddenly he fancied the water was thickening in colour. It was a brilliant day, without a sign of rain. He looked over his shoulder up the river, and about 150 or 200 yards off he saw a big red wave, a regular bore about five or six feet high, coming down like a racehorse. Not a moment was to be lost, and he bolted for the landing place as hard as his legs could carry him, and he only just reached it, for the little stream which was not over his ankles five minutes before was up to his waist before he got out of it, and in another half minute an elephant would have been carried away in it. I was nearly caught once in the same way on the upper part of the Coquet. I mention these facts that anglers may be aware of them when they are fishing Highland rivers.
The accompanying patterns I obtained from Sir Alexander, who was one of the best amateur tyers in the North, and it is but a few years since that I enjoyed the pleasure of his hospitality in his beautiful residence on the banks of the lovely Findhorn. We fished, tied flies, and held sweet converse upon matters piscatorial, and I have seldom enjoyed a week more thoroughly than I spent at Altyre. He was then apparently in the

prime of his strength and the prime of manhood. How beautifully he tied the salmon fly, blending its colours into one harmonious combination, and with what a workmanlike and skilful hand he hurled it across the water.

The Findhorn spring flies are rather large and showy – not so large as the Dee flies, perhaps, but full large, some of the flies (the largest) being dressed on the ordinary Limerick hook, from No. 2 to No. 5. In low water they may be used smaller than this.
Here are Sir Alexander's patterns.

No. 1

Tag	Gold thread and puce floss.
Tail	A good-sized topping, some tippet, and a kingfisher feather.
Butt	Black ostrich herl.
Body	Lightish claret floss.
Rib	Silver tinsel and gold twist (not together but equidistant).
Hackle	Light claret to match the body.
Shoulder	Blue jay.
Wings	Two large tippet feathers, almost the length of the hook, over them sprigs of golden pheasant tail, a good many sprigs of blue and red macaw, slips of gled (kite) and dark bustard. On either side, nearly half the length of the wing, the tips of two blue macaw feathers.
Head	The head is composed of orange mohair, set on like a hackle, and forming a ruff. (Most of the Findhorn flies are mounted in this way and it makes them very conspicuous. In some Sir Alexander used the soft silky *Pinna marina*, and it had a very striking effect.)
Hooks	2 or 3

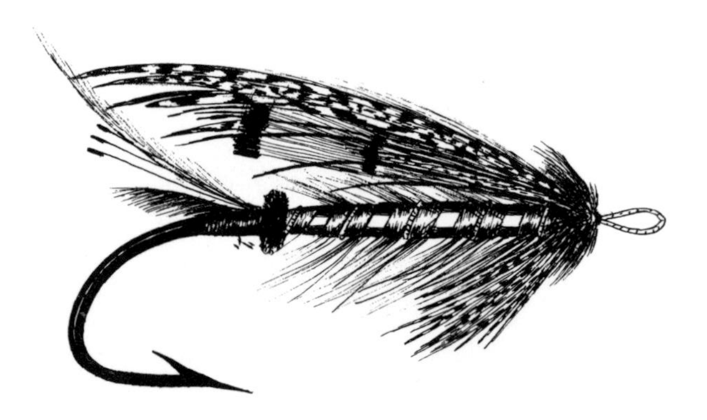

Sir Alexander's No. 1

No. 2

Tag	Silver thread and yellow floss.
Tail	A good sized topping, some tippet and gallina.
Butt	Black ostrich herl.
Body	Copper-coloured floss.
Rib	Broad silver tinsel and narrow gold tinsel, side by side.
Hackle	Medium claret.
Shoulder	Blue jay.
Wings	Two tippet feathers (a little shorter than No. 1), a little English bustard, brown mallard, brown speckled turkey, bright bustard, red macaw and pale green swan sprigs.
Head	Black.
Hooks	3 or 4

No. 3

Tag	Silver thread and ruby floss.
Tail	A good-sized topping and tippet.
Butt	Black ostrich herl.
Body	Orange-yellow floss.
Rib	Broad gold tinsel.
Hackle	Light blue.
Shoulder	Blue jay.
Wings	One medium-sized tippet, two good slices of brown speckled turkey, sprigs of golden pheasant tail, and a few red, and blue macaw fibres.
Ruff	Bright red mohair (head).
Horns	Blue macaw, tied in over the ruff.
Hooks	3 or 4

No. 4

Tag	Silver tinsel.
Tail	One good topping.

Body Three turns of ruby floss, the rest of light apple-green floss.
Rib Silver and gold tinsel side by side.
Hackle Bright medium green, inclined to a blue-green.
Shoulder Black heron hackle, the fibres reaching the barb of the hook.
Wings A bunch of emerald-green peacock herl (taken from the scimitar-shaped feather), slices of brown speckled turkey, bright peacock, a little bustard, red and blue macaw and green swan.
Ruff Blue mohair (head).
Hooks 4 or 5

No. 5
Tag Silver thread and a small bunch of red mohair.
Tail A topping and some tippet, sprigs of golden pheasant sword feather, blue macaw and pale yellow-green parrot.
Butt Black ostrich herl.
Body Three turns of ruby floss, the rest of light apple-green floss (a shade lighter than No. 4).
Rib Gold and silver tinsel, side by side.
Hackle Coch-y-bonddu, stained brown.
Shoulder Black heron, reaching the point of the hook.
Wings Strips of bustard and bright peacock, sprigs of blue, and red macaw and yellow-green swan.
Ruff Bright orange mohair (head).
Hooks 4 or 5

No. 6
Tag Silver thread and yellow floss.
Tail A long topping, tippet, and a red toucan feather.
Butt Black ostrich herl.
Body Black floss.
Rib Silver tinsel and gold thread, side by side.
Hackle A dark chocolate-brown cock's feather.
Shoulder Black heron with gallina over it.
Wings Two tippet feathers (two-thirds the length of the wing); mixed peacock and golden pheasant tail, with fibres of red and blue macaw over.
Ruff Olive yellow mohair (head).
Hook 4

No. 7
Tag Gold thread.
Tail A topping and some gallina.
Body One turn of orange-yellow pig's wool, then two of light claret-red, two of medium blue, three of clarety-red, and three of orange-yellow.
Rib Broadish gold tinsel.
Hackle Dark purple.
Shoulder Black hackle with blue jay over it.
Wings One tippet (half the length of the wing), mixed golden pheasant tail, mallard, a little gallina, a little bright bustard, a few sprigs of long tippet, and of yellow and claret swan, and several blue macaw sprigs.
Head (No ruff.) Black.
Hook 5

No. 8
Tag Silver thread and dark blue floss.
Tail A good topping.
Butt Black ostrich herl.
Body One-third orange-yellow floss, the rest dark chocolate floss.
Rib None.
Hackle A brown claret.
Shoulder Black heron (shortish).
Wings A long tippet, the tip of a black partridge feather, a bit of dark brown mallard, and the tip of a green parrot feather; over this sprigs of brown turkey, golden pheasant tail, two or three copper-coloured peacock herls, red, and blue macaw.
Cheeks Kingfisher.
Ruff Mohair (not too heavy), the colour of which is not orange or pink, but a sort of madder.
Hook 5, a trifle shorter than the last.

Sir Alexander gave some directions for varying the flies, and I cannot do better than append his letter.

Altyre, Forres, N.B., July 30, 1865.

My Dear Sir, – I have selected eight of the flies which I have found most killing on the Findhorn, during twenty years work. These may be successfully varied by changing the colour of the bodies and heads; red for orange, black for yellow heads, and bodies made black for claret or green, and *vice versa*. These eight patterns I generally adhere to throughout the year, by dressing them one, two, and three sizes smaller. Blue bodies may be substituted in the case of the black and two clarets, with advantage to the angler and detriment to the fish. The wings of two are far too long, but this you need not mind. *All* should have one or two toppings (shortish) for tails, and if the wing is *dressed thinner* it is an *immense* improvement, where economy is no object, to put two long toppings on the wing.

Yours truly,

A. P. Gordon Cumming

THE TAY

The Tay is a splendid river. The water is heavy, but some of the pools and streams are magnificent. The fishing on the lower part of the river is mostly from a boat, and the style is called 'harling'. Three rods are used and the boat is rowed to and fro over the casts. Two of the rods usually have a couple of flies on each, and the third a phantom minnow, and it was not an uncommon thing for two of the rods to have a fish on at the same moment, and I have even heard an instance or two of all three of them being at work simultaneously. A few of the casts, however, can be fished from the shore, and where this is the case, the sport is of a very superior kind; for owing to the size of the river and weight of the stream, Tay fish nearly always show great sport. The Tay has been rendered famous by poor Leech, as it was on one of the best known parts of the river that the immortal Briggs killed the great salmon. A magnificent piece of water it is, and is known by the euphonious title of Hell Hole.

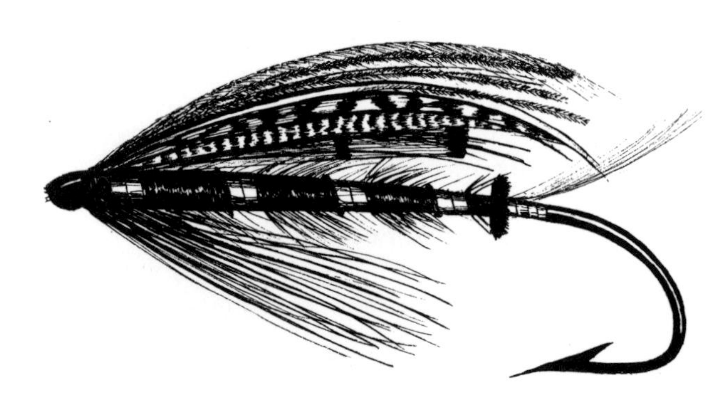

The Black Dog

The system of letting fishing on the Tay is a capital one as it provides fishing for a large number of persons at a moderate outlay, while the total of rents is considerable. It is customary to take a certain water for one special day per week throughout the season, five other persons taking the other five days, each lessee fishing it in turn. The river is best in summer and autumn; gives a few fish in the spring, but the best sport is in the autumn.

The spring flies for the Tay are of the largest size, three inches and longer being used on heavy water, but a good moderate size for the upper parts of the Tay would be dressed on hooks of No. 4 and 5 as per my hook scale.

Mr Paton of Perth, who is the highest authority on such matters, gives the following patterns.

The Black Dog *Colour plate 5*

This fly, like all the other Tay flies, has over the past few years undergone a thorough revolution. All the old plain wings, the long slips of dun turkey and gold have disappeared, and in their stead mixed wings with jungle-cock, wood-duck, and toppings in them reign. Mr Paton remarks in his letter to me upon the change . . . 'Even the very Wasps and Black Dog, old standard flies since the memory of the oldest inhabitant, now no longer tak' their auld cloaks about them.'

Tag	Silver tinsel.
Tail	A topping.
Butt	Black ostrich herl.
Body	Black floss.
Rib	Silver and gold tinsel and red silk, side by side.

Hackle Black, all the way up.
Shoulder A very long-fibred heron's hackle dyed blue.
Wings A mixed wing. The under wing is a tippet feather with slices of wood-duck over. The over wing is mixed fibres of golden pheasant tail, bustard, claret, yellow, and orange swan, speckled peacock and some peacock herls, blue, and red macaw, and a topping over all.
Head Black.
Hooks 4 or 5, 3 inches, or longer.

The Claret Wasp

This fly has also undergone a similar transformation.

Tag Gold tinsel.
Tail A topping and a turn of orange or dirty red wool.
Body One-third of dirty yellow wool, one-third claret, and one-third dark blue picked out at the shoulder.
Rib Silver tinsel.
Hackle Rusty coch-y-bonddu.
Shoulder Gallina.
Wings Golden pheasant tail, bustard, claret, and orange swan, a slice of tippet, pintail, a slip of wood-duck either side and a topping over all.
Horns Blue macaw.
Head Black.
Hooks 4 or 5

The Black Wasp

Tag Gold tinsel.
Tail A topping and a turn of orange or dirty red wool.
Body Half dirty yellow wool, and half black wool.
Rib Embossed gold tinsel over the yellow wool, and silver tinsel over the black wool.
Hackle A dirty yellow olive hackle over the yellow wool, and a black hackle over the black wool.
Shoulder Blue jay.
Wings Golden pheasant tail, bustard, claret and orange swan, tippet fibres, pintail, shortish jungle-cock on either side and a topping over all.
Head Black.
Hooks 4 or 5

The Blue Wasp *Colour plate 5*

Tag Gold twist.
Tail A topping.
Butt Black ostrich herl.
Body Lower half, reddish orange wool (roughish). Upper half, dark blue wool.
Rib Gold thread over lower half, silver tinsel and silver twist over upper half.
Hackle A dark mauve (more of a violet-coloured) hackle over the blue wool.
Shoulder Gallina.
Wings Golden pheasant tail, bustard, fibres of claret, blue, and orange swan, a slice of tippet, pintail, a slip of wood-duck either side and a topping over all.
Horns Blue macaw.
Head Black.
Hooks 4 or 5

The Tay Tartan

Tag Silver tinsel.
Tail A topping, fibres of claret hackle and black partridge.
Butt Scarlet wool.
Body In seven joints of dirty yellow, orange, dark red, claret, darkish blue, claret again and then black; each of wool.
Rib Silver tinsel and gold thread.
Hackle A black hackle all the way up.
Shoulder A reddish orange hackle with gallina over it.
Wings Under wing, two tippet feathers. Over, a good deal of grey speckled peacock, a little bustard, a few claret, orange, yellow and blue swan sprigs, and some pintail over.
Head Black.
Hooks 4 or 5

The Royal *Colour plate 5*

Tag Silver tinsel and ruby floss.
Tail A topping and a bit of ibis.
Butt Black ostrich herl.
Body One-third oval gold twist, at the joint an orange-yellow hackle with claret ostrich herl over it; then two-thirds of medium light blue silk.
Hackle See above.
Rib Silver tinsel and silver twist over the blue silk.
Shoulder Jay, with a long-fibred blue hackle over, same shade as body.
Wings Golden pheasant tail, bustard, pintail; claret, yellow, and orange swan, a slice of wood-duck in the middle, and two short jungle-cock feathers at the sides. A topping over all.
Head Claret ostrich herl.
Hooks 4 or 5

The Scottish Shannon

I am afraid that as we have a Shannon later on we must make a sort of bull and call this the Scottish Shannon. It is rather a whim.

Tag Silver tinsel.
Tail A topping.
Butt Black ostrich herl.
Body Floss silk in five joints: yellow-orange, pink, claret, blue, and a double length of a lighter blue.
Rib Broadish silver tinsel spiralled over each joint.
Hackle A dark red coch-y-bonddu hackle all the way up.
Shoulder A medium blue hackle with black over it.
Wings Under wing, short tippet feathers. Over wing, golden pheasant tail, grey speckled peacock, claret-orange, and yellow swan, over that wood-duck (the part without the black bars), short jungle-cock over that, and a topping over all.
Head Black.
Hooks 4 or 5

The Dunkeld

With these Mr Paton says that the Blue Doctor, the Dusty Miller and Jock Scott are general favourites. To these I add the following patterns sent to me by Roderick Anderson, of Dunkeld – and a very superior tyer he is.

The Yellow Wasp

One of the handsomest of his race.

Tag Silver twist.
Tail A topping, an Indian crow feather, fibres of black partridge, ibis and tippet.
Butt Black ostrich herl.
Body Lower half yellow and upper half medium blue pig's wool.
Rib Narrow gold tinsel over the yellow half and medium silver over the blue.
Hackle A blue hackle over the upper half the same shade as the wool, and a black hackle over that.
Shoulder Blue jay.
Wings A pair of dun turkey with whitish tips.
Head Black.
Hooks 4 or 5

The Dunkeld

A warm handsome fly.

Tag Silver tinsel and pale blue floss.
Tail A topping and some wood-duck (without the black and white tips) or grey mallard.
Butt Black ostrich herl.

Body	Three turns of yellow orange floss, the rest of brighter orange pig's wool.
Rib	Broad silver tinsel.
Hackle	Orange hackle the same shade as the pig's wool all the way up.
Shoulder	Pale blue hackle.
Wings	Under wing, some black partridge and wood-duck. Over wing, dark turkey with a white tip; over this, fibres of green peacock, golden pheasant, and blue, red, and yellow swan.
Horns	Blue macaw.
Head	Black.
Hooks	4 or 5

The Lord James Murray

Tag	Silver twist and orange floss.
Tail	A topping and a kingfisher's feather.
Butt	Black ostrich herl.
Body	Black floss silk.
Rib	Broad silver tinsel and silver twist.
Hackle	A black hackle (sparse) all the way up.
Shoulder	Black heron (to reach the hook point) with an orange hackle over it.
Wings	Under wing, tippet. Over wing, slips of wood-duck, golden pheasant tail, pintail, mallard, bustard, and green, and red swan.
Head	Black.
Hooks	4 or 5

The Fancy Olive

This is also a nice looking fly.

Tag	Silver twist.
Tail	A topping, some black partridge, tippet, and a short jungle-cock.
Butt	Black ostrich herl.
Body	Two turns of golden olive floss, then golden olive pig's wool, and a little reddish orange pig's wool at the shoulder.
Rib	Broad silver tinsel and silver twist.
Hackle	Golden olive, same shade as pig's wool.
Shoulder	Gallina.
Wings	Dark turkey with white tips, fibres of green peacock, golden pheasant tail, blue, red and yellow swan. (Similar to that of the Dunkeld, (p.34) only no under wing.)
Head	Black.
Hooks	4 or 5

One more fly and we must close the list for the Tay.

The Plain Shannon *Colour plate 5*

Why so called I don't know; it is not a bit like other Shannons.

Tag	Silver twist.
Tail	A tuft of bright golden mohair, and over it a topping, some tippet, ibis, and black partridge sprigs.
Butt	Black ostrich herl.
Body	In four joints of yellow, orange, red, and blue pig's wool, rough and picked out; a sort of Namsen body.
Rib	Silver twist and silver tinsel.
Hackle	Black heron's hackle extending to the point of the hook.
Shoulder	Blue jay.
Wings	A pair of dark dun turkey feathers with lightish tips.
Head	Black.
Hooks	4 or 5

Mr Anderson also sends the Black Dog, the Dusty Miller, the Butcher, and the Major.

THE TUMMEL, GARRY AND ISLA

The best fly for these rivers is the Blue Doctor dressed with a very light blue body, with a blue jay and gallina hackle at the shoulders. The Black and Teal and the Fancy Olive are good but the Doctor is the favourite and should be kept in two or three sizes. Here are three patterns I got at Pitlochry:

No. 1

Tag Fine silver twist and gold floss.
Tail A topping.
Butt Reddish brown ostrich herl.
Body Rough pig's wool (picked out) of dark red, dark blue, then dark red, and dark blue again alternately.
Rib Silver tinsel and gold thread alternately (not together).
Shoulder (No body hackle.) Two turns of brick-dust red hackle and two turns of jay over.
Wings Golden pheasant tail, pintail, tippet, a sprig or two of blue or yellow swan, two slices of mallard, and one topping over all.
Head Black.
Hook 6

No. 2

Tag Fine silver twist and gold floss.
Tail A topping.
Butt Black ostrich herl.
Body Pig's wool, half of darkish red, the other half dark blue.
Rib Silver tinsel and fine gold twist together.
Hackle Lightish blue hackle over the blue joint only.
Shoulder Two turns of jay.
Wings Grey speckled peacock wing, tippet, a sprig or two of blue and yellow swan, two slices of mallard, and a few fibres of orange, and red swan. A topping over all.
Head Black.
Hook 6

No. 3

Tag Fine silver twist and gold floss.
Tail A topping.
Butt Black ostrich herl.
Body The darkest blue pig's wool.
Rib Silver tinsel and fine gold thread alternately, (not together).
Hackle Black all the way up.
Shoulder Two turns of jay.
Wings Chiefly brown mallard, with some red, yellow, blue, and orange fibres, and a little pintail under it.
Head Black.
Hook 6

THE LYON

The Lyon joins the Tay just below Taymouth. It is a pretty river and sometimes yields good sport. The flies are not too thick in the body and are somewhat of the wasp pattern.

No. 1

Tag Silver tinsel.
Tail A topping and a piece of tippet.
Butt None.
Body Lower half dirty yellow pig's wool, the upper half a very dark red pig's wool with a slight claret tinge in it.
Rib Silver tinsel.
Hackle Black over the red pig's wool.
Shoulder A grouse hackle.
Wings Large spot gallina, and lightish speckled turkey over it.
Head Black.
Hook 6

No. 2

Tag Silver tinsel.
Tail Tippet.
Butt Black ostrich herl.
Body Lower half dirty yellow pig's wool, the upper half dark blue pig's wool.
Rib Silver tinsel.
Hackle Dark claret over the blue pig's wool.
Shoulder A few turns of jay.
Wings Rich brown turkey.
Head Black.
Hook 6

No. 3

Tag	Gold thread and ruby floss.
Tail	Tippet and a scrap of dark blue pig's wool.
Butt	Black ostrich herl.
Body	Yellow pig's wool merging into orange, then into claret, and then again into black.
Rib	Gold thread.
Hackle	Black hackle over the black pig's wool.
Shoulder	A few turns of jay.
Wings	A slip of orange-stained turkey, and rich brown turkey (unspeckled at the points) over.
Head	Black.
Hook	6

These are useful flies on the Tay or anywhere else in low water.

THE EARN

These patterns I also received from Mr Paton who says that tastes have changed less on the Earn of late years than on the Tay. The wings are put on in a way that makes one envious, for it is not easy to put on slips of turkey artistically. Mr Paton's tyer is evidently a dab at it, and I have made a note to take a lesson from him when I go Northward again. First Mr Paton sends the invariable three wasps.

No. 1 Wasp

Tag	Silver tinsel and orange-yellow floss.
Tail	Tippet, gallina and black partridge.
Butt	Black ostrich herl.
Body	Lower half dirty yellow pig's wool, the upper half dark blue pig's wool.
Rib	Embossed gold tinsel over lower half and silver tinsel over upper half.
Hackle	Golden-olive hackle over the yellow wool, and black over the blue wool.
Shoulder	Two or three turns of jay.
Wings	Two slips of brown speckled turkey.
Head	Black.
Hook	6

No. 2 Wasp

Just like No. 1, only the upper joint of the body is black instead of blue, and the tail is yellow wool and tippet.

No. 3 Wasp

Tag	Silver twist.
Tail	Dark red pig's wool and a topping.
Butt	Black ostrich herl.
Body	Lower half orange-red, upper half dark blue pig's wool.
Rib	Gold thread over the red joint, and narrow embossed silver tinsel over the blue.
Hackle	Dark blue hackle over the blue wool.
Shoulder	A few turns of jay.
Wings	Again the wings are two slips of brown speckled turkey.
Head	Black.
Hooks	8 or 9

Then come three flies without names.

Mr Paton's No. 1 (Wasp)

No. 1

Tag	Silver tinsel.
Tail	Yellow wool and a topping.
Butt	Black ostrich herl.
Body	Dark red pig's wool.
Rib	Silver tinsel and gold thread alternately.
Hackle	Common red hackle all the way up.
Shoulder	A few turns of jay.
Wings	Cinnamon dun turkey.
Head	Black.
Hook	6

No. 2

Tag	Silver tinsel.
Tail	A wad of orange crewel with a few sprigs of saddle feather from a golden pheasant over it.
Butt	Black ostrich herl.
Body	In five joints of yellow, orange, claret, red, and dark blue pig's wool.
Rib	Silver tinsel.
Hackle	A red cock's hackle with a black centre, all the way up the body.
Shoulder	Two turns of darkest gallina.
Wings	Dark rich cinnamon dun turkey with light tips.
Head	Black.
Hook	6

No. 3

Just like the last except that it has a brown speckled turkey wing. Hook No. 6.

Then comes a fly called:

The Olive

Tag	Silver tinsel, and a wad of yellow wool picked out and left rough all round the bend of the hook.
Tail	Black partridge, yellow and red parrot.
Butt	Black ostrich herl.
Body	Dirty yellow wool.
Rib	Broad silver and narrow gold tinsel alternately.
Hackle	Dark olive all the way up.
Shoulder	A few turns of jay.
Wings	Two slips of brown speckled turkey.
Head	Black.
Hooks	6 (round bend).

THE TEITH

The Honourable W. Drummond procured for me the following patterns, he being an old frequenter of the Teith.

No. 1

Tag	Silver tinsel and lemon floss.
Tail	A topping
Butt	Black ostrich herl.
Body	Silver tinsel.
Rib	Silver twist.
Shoulder	(No body hackle.) A bit of scarlet wool tied in at shoulder and picked out, with a black hackle over.
Wings	A mixed wing of emerald peacock, claret, and yellow swan, tippet and grey drake, and slips of mallard over.
Head	Black.
Hooks	6–10

No. 2

This is also an old Tweed pattern.

Tag	None.
Tail	Tippet.
Body	In five joints of yellow, orange, red, claret, and black wool.
Rib	Broad silver tinsel and gold twist.
Hackle	A coch-y-bonddu hackle with a good black stump to it, starting half-way along body and ending on shoulder.
Wings	Cinnamon turkey with light tip.
Head	Black.
Hooks	6–10

Mr Drummond then sends four from Mr Cameron of Blair Drummond, a very good authority.

No. 1

Tag	Gold tinsel, then one turn of bright yellow crewel with a short slip of it left for a rudimentary tail.
Tail	See above.
Butt	One turn of scarlet wool.
Body	Light blue wool with the faintest tinge of green in it, one turn of yellow wool at the shoulder.
Rib	Medium silver tinsel.
Hackle	A grizzled blue dun hackle with a blackish stump to it, all the way up and at shoulder.
Wings	From the streaky feather in a golden pheasant tail.
Head	Black.
Hooks	5–10, to suit the season, the larger numbers in spring and the smallest in summer.

No. 2

Tag	Gold tinsel.
Tail	A bit of crimson, and yellow crewel.
Body	Clarety red (approaching to lake) wool, a turn of yellow wool at the shoulder.
Rib	Medium silver tinsel.
Hackle	A grizzled blue dun hackle as before but darker with more black in the centre and stump, all the way up the body and ending on the shoulder.
Wings	Rich brown turkey with black bars and nearly white tip.
Head	Black.
Hooks	5–10

No. 3

Tag	Silver tinsel and gold floss.
Tail	A topping.
Butt	Black ostrich herl.
Body	Nearly half bright yellow, the rest lightish medium blue wool, picked out.
Rib	Broad gold tinsel.
Shoulder	(No body hackle.) Gallina hackle.

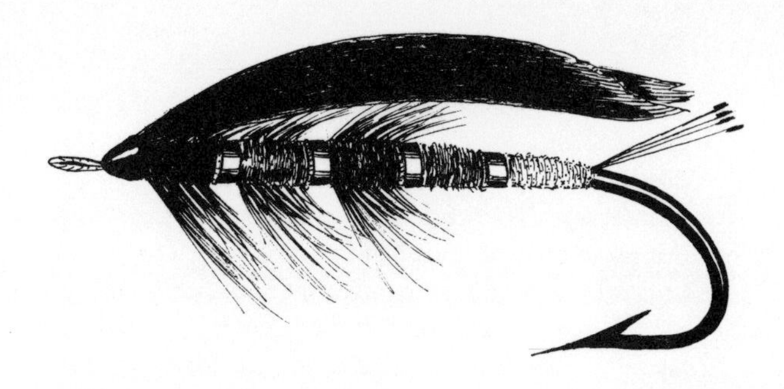

The Hon. W. Drummond's No. 2

Wings	Sprigs of rich brown turkey and black partridge, yellow, red, and lavender swan, and slips of brown mallard over, and a topping over all.
Cheeks	Jungle cock.
Head	Black.
Hooks	5–10

No. 4

This is the Britannia with a bright orange body; hackle of the same, and a violet hackle as a ruff over the wing.

The Jock Scott may be added to the above list.

THE FORTH

With respect to the Forth, Lord Strathallan, Mr Drummond's father, to whom he very kindly wrote for information as to the Forth flies, says in his reply that 'The flies for the Forth are much like those for the Tay and Earn, which Paton of Perth is the best provider of. The fish take a very large fly in the spring; long grey heron hackle, with blue pig's wool, and a red dub is very good for snow water or a grey day. In cold weather fish deep in the water.' The last piece of advice of Lord Strathallan's is exceedingly good, and is applicable to more waters than the Forth.

THE SPEY

The Spey is another magnificent river which often gives grand sport. The river is large and the angling is mostly from the banks which are frequently high, while the stream is not only heavy but often tremendously rapid and rough, as is the bottom; therefore, an indifferent fisherman cannot expect much sport on the Spey. It is a very long river, having many mountainous tributaries and thus it often keeps up and out of condition for fishing for a much longer time than is agreeable to the angler. This is frequently the case in spring when the snows on the mountains are melting, and when sport to any extent cannot be relied on. After the great bulk of the snow is gone in the early summer, when the river is settling steadily down and the grilse are beginning to come up, is perhaps the best time for the Spey.
The Spey flies are very curious productions to look at. It is customary to dress them the reverse way of the hackle, and to wind the rib the opposite way to the hackle.

The Spey Dog
This is usually dressed large for the spring, the long-shanked Dee hooks being preferred; it has no tag, tail, or butt.

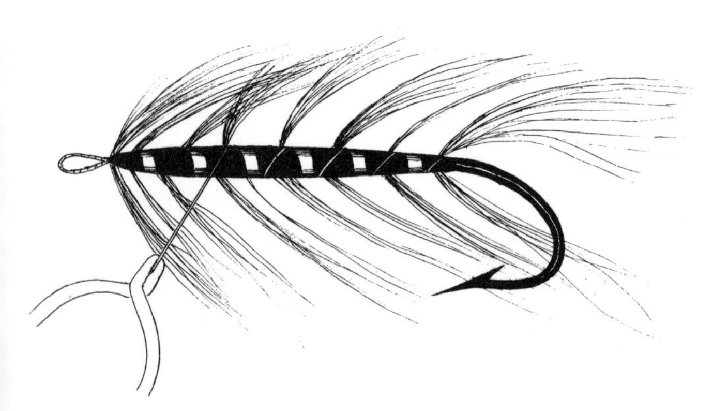

The second rib of the Spey Fly: in tying this type of Spey fly, the hackle is wound on from tail to head, starting with the widest end of the hackle.

Body	Black pig's wool.
1st rib	Broad silver tinsel in widish rings.
Hackle	Over the tinsel is laid on a large black feather (it can hardly be called a hackle) with a lightish dun tip, taken from the side of a Scotch cock's tail. This feather is dressed the wrong way so that the hackle stands out abruptly, and is carried round the opposite way to the tinsel, as some of the tinsel crosses it.
2nd rib	Over the hackle is wound some gold tinsel, not side by side with the silver, but quite independent of it. This aids the glitter of the fly and strengthens and keeps the hackle secure. (See illustration.)
Shoulder	A teal hackle.
Wings	A good wad of golden pheasant tail, with two long strips of grey mallard with brownish points over it.
Head	As with the Dee flies no head is formed, the fibres being tied in tight at the butt.
Hooks	The hook used in these flies is 3 inches long in the shank, and the bend is that given as No. 3 in the scale, but which is barely $2\frac{1}{4}$ inches long in the shank.

The Purple King *Colour plate 5*
This is tied in a similar fashion to the Spey Dog.

Body	A light purple mohair.
1st rib	Gold and silver tinsel in widish rings.
Hackle	A brownish black feather with light blue dun tip.
2nd rib	Silver twist, over hackle as before.
Wings	Two strips of grey mallard with brown stripes.
Head	As before.
Hooks	Again as before.

The Green King
The body is orange and olive-yellow mixed mohair. The hackle is brown with grey tips; the rest of the fly is the same as the Purple King.

For these last two patterns I am indebted to my friend Mr C. Grant of Aberlour. Mr Grant very kindly furnished me with minute particulars as to the dressing, dyeing, etc. and I cannot put his directions in a better form than he has put them himself, and therefore, I append his letter. In it he describes two other flies I had not the patterns of, viz. the Green Dog and Purby. They are well known standard flies on the Spey, and may be dressed down to the smallest size for midsummer; the Black and Teal already described will be found very hard to beat on the Spey.

Dear Sir, – Agreeably to my promise, I now send you the pattern Spey flies, viz. two Purple Kings and one Green King, which you will easily distinguish. The hackles are got from the common *Scotch cock*, and lie on each side of the tail, at the tip of the wings. The cock is rarely to be met with except with Spey fishers, who breed them for the sake of their feathers. The dubbing or 'grounds' of the Purple King are composed of purple (Berlin wool), stone red, dyed from the moss on stones, and scarlet wool. The dubbing of Green King is composed of green Berlin wool, stone red, yellow, a little orange and scarlet.

In spring the Purple King is of a less red colour than one used at present. The Green King at that period is more *green*, but, as the season advances more red is used in both, and redder feathers. I enclose some dubbing of each to fit the present season.

Without having any prejudice against *gaudy flies*, I would prefer Purple and Green Kings with their *numerous offspring*, providing I could get proper hackles to tie them, to any flies that can be used on the Spey. The flies which I have sent you will be in size next month (July), and I have no doubt that they will *kill* upon any river in Scotland.

The dubbing of Green Dog is the same as Green King, feather a little lighter, with gold coloured spate and pea-green thread at equal distances on the body of the hook or fly. The Purple, or 'Purpy', a thirty-second cousin of the Purple King, has a hackle somewhat redder than that of his progenitor; dubbing, dark blue and stone red, with gold spate and purple thread on body of fly at equal distances.

C. Grant

LOCH LOMOND

The salmon flies for Loch Lomond do not run very large. It is seldom much before July or August that sport with salmon is to be had in the loch, and then the portion of water between Balloch and Luss is the best part. They are all dressed very roughly with hackle only at the shoulder, and all have the finest silver twist ribs. Very few of them have tails and when they have it is only a tuft of yellow pig's wool. The wings are of widgeon or pintail, dun turkey with light tip, or brown mallard.

No. 1

Tail	A tuft of yellow pig's wool.
Body	Darkish orange wool.
Rib	Silver twist.
Shoulder	A brownish red hackle, dark at the butt.
Wings	Dun turkey.
Head	Black.
Hooks	7–9

No. 2

Body	Orange wool, a shade lighter than No. 1.
Rib	Silver twist.
Shoulder	A brownish red hackle, a shade lighter than No. 1.
Wings	Dun turkey, same as No. 1.
Head	Black.
Hooks	7–9

No. 3

Body	Yellow wool.
Rib	Silver twist.
Shoulder	A brownish red hackle, dark at the butt.
Wings	Mallard.
Head	Black.
Hooks	7–9

No. 4

Body	Yellow wool a shade lighter than No. 3, getting towards lemon.
Rib	Silver twist.
Shoulder	Black hackle.
Wings	Widgeon.
Head	Black.
Hooks	7–9

No. 5

Body	Medium green wool with a slight mixture of yellow fibres in it.
Rib	Silver twist.
Shoulder	Red hackle.
Wings	Widgeon.
Head	Black.
Hooks	7–9

No. 6

Body	The same as No. 5.
Rib	Silver twist.
Shoulder	Brownish red hackle, dark at the butt.
Wings	Mallard.
Head	Black.
Hooks	7–9

No. 7

Body	Two-fifths yellow and three-fifths clarety red wool.
Rib	Silver twist.
Shoulder	A long-fibred furnace hackle dyed claret.
Wings	Dun turkey with light tip.
Head	Black.
Hooks	7–9

No. 8

Body	Almost the same as No. 7, but the red more scarlet.
Rib	Silver twist.
Shoulder	A longish-fibred black hackle.
Wings	Dun turkey.
Head	Black.
Hooks	7–9

No. 9

Body	As before, but the red a trifle lighter still.
Rib	Silver twist.
Shoulder	A brownish red hackle, dark at the butt but longer in the fibre than No. 1.
Wings	Widgeon.
Head	Black.
Hooks	7–9

No. 10

Body	Two-fifths yellow and three-fifths dark orange wool.
Rib	Silver twist.
Shoulder	Black hackle.
Wings	Widgeon.
Head	Black.
Hooks	7–9

No. 11

Body	Lower half yellow, the upper half medium blue wool.
Rib	Silver twist.
Shoulder	Longish-blue hackle.
Wings	Mallard.
Head	Black.
Hooks	7–9

No. 12

Body	Same as No. 11, a trifle brighter blue.
Rib	Silver twist.
Shoulder	Blue hackle.
Wings	Dun turkey.
Head	Black.
Hooks	7–9

Chapter Three

Flies for Irish Rivers and Loughs

THE ERNE

The Parson

The Parson has already been described amongst the general flies, but since I described it I have received some patterns along with a letter from my friend Dr Shiel, the former kind and liberal proprietor of the Erne, to whom I owe many favours for some excellent fishing on one of the finest rivers on which it has ever been my lot to cast a fly. For the Erne is the beau-ideal of a salmon river, containing every kind of water that is found in salmon rivers, and all in perfection. Here we have falls, rapids, broken pools, rocky torrents, and swift glassy currents, and even heavy reaches for boat fishing. The fish run large and nearly always show the finest sport. The sport is best in the months of June and July, if the river is low enough, for it is much more apt to be too high than too low, running as it does from such a very large water as Lough Erne. The river is very rarely too low for sport, and even in the hottest and brightest weather sport is possible. The river is now held by a company who let it out in rods by the week. As Dr Shiel's letter gives the history of the Parson, I give here his letter.

My dear Sir, – I send four Parsons I have borrowed from Mr Hobson, and I will send you a couple made with summer duck in the wing. The first 'Parson' and called from him, was used by the Rev. Alfred Meyrick of Romsbury; it was two large toppings, a yellow body, yellow hackle, very thin twist run close together up the body – I mean half as close as in any of those flies I send. He said he got it from Lord Bolingbroke at Christchurch. He changed the body to orange; both were silk bodies.

The late Mr William Larket of Derby, put cock of the rock in the wing. I think I put the first fur body to the fly – it was orange pig's wool. Mr Larket and then Mr Hobson altered the fur to a mixture of red and yellow. Mr Hobson added to this the purple and fiery brown under the wing, which Pat McKay borrowed and adopted, and nothing has beaten this pattern.

Yours,

S. Shiel

The flies sent are all very similar to the patterns already described, save that some of them have in the wing strips of summer or wood-duck, as it is more commonly termed, instead of pintail. Some have merely the toppings and two cock of the rock feathers in the wing. Most of them have longish kingfisher feathers at the cheek. Some have and some have not the bit of tippet for an under wing. Some, instead of jay, have a medium blue hackle at shoulder, and some a claret hackle. In these latter cases, the hackle is dressed outside or over the wing, the horns put on over that; these are macaw where the blue feather changes to red at the points. The tags vary a little, some being puce, some orange and some yellow silk. The bodies vary slightly from yellow pig's wool to yellow with little or more orange. One of them has a brown body, but I do not much like it. The hackles run from golden to golden-olive and orange. It will thus be seen that a Parson may be as varied as his creeds are: he may be a gorgeous ritualist or a plain parson Adams.

Mr Rogan's Erne patterns

I sent to Mike Rogan of Ballyshannon, one of the prettiest fly-tyers in Ireland, to lend me a few patterns from the Erne, and he sent the following:

No. 1

Tag Silver twist and darkish blue floss.
Tail A topping and sprigs of tippet and wood-duck and a small Indian crow feather.
Butt None.
Body Medium orange floss.
Rib Silver tinsel and doubled silver thread.
Hackle An orange hackle a shade or two redder than the body, all the way up.
Shoulder A turn or two of medium blue hackle.
Wings A few tippet and peacock sword feather fibres with one or two of dark wood-duck. Over them golden pheasant tail and two toppings over all.
Cheeks Kingfisher.
Horns Blue macaw.
Head Black.
Hook 6

A very pretty, and I am sure effective, fly.

No. 2

Tag Silver twist and orange floss.
Tail A topping and sprigs of tippet and wood-duck with a small Indian crow feather at the stump (same as No. 1).
Butt None.
Body One turn of yellowish orange wool, the rest of a dirty reddish claret. I hardly know how to describe this colour which I believe is got from crottle dye.
Rib Silver thread and gold tinsel together.
Hackle The same colour as the body all the way up. Springs of tippet are tied in pretty full at the breast.
Shoulder A medium blue hackle over the tippet sprigs mentioned above.
Wings Two of the longest Indian crow feathers and tippet sprigs over them; over that, a shred or two of dark wood-duck and golden pheasant tail followed by two strips of wood-duck with a topping between them.
Cheeks Kingfisher.
Horns Blue macaw.
Head Black.
Hook 6

No. 3

Tag Silver twist and orange floss, and one turn of medium blue floss.
Tail A topping and sprigs of tippet and wood-duck and a small Indian crow feather (as before).
Body (again no butt) All of pig's wool starting with one turn of dirty yellow, two of orange, merging into a dirty reddish claret (as described in No. 2) the wool is then picked out.
Rib Silver thread.
Hackle A dirty orange (a shade lighter than in No. 2) all the way up. I believe this shade is also got from crottle. These crottle colours are difficult to describe and unless the tyer got them from Rogan I should fear he would find it difficult to hit them.
Shoulder Two turns of medium blue hackle with a claret hackle over.
Wings Two of the longest Indian crow feathers and tippet sprigs over them; over that, a shred or two of dark wood-duck and golden pheasant tail followed by two strips of wood-duck with three toppings between them. A similar wing to No. 2 but with three toppings instead of one.
Horns Blue macaw.
Head Black.
Hook 5

The next two flies are well-tried favourites which I should never be without on the Erne. With No. 4 I have at long intervals killed many good fish on the Erne. A fish once went up the second fall with me and came down with this fly in his mouth.

No. 4

Tag Silver twist and medium blue floss.
Tail A topping.
Butt Black ostrich herl.
Body Three turns of light orange floss, the rest of light purple. This is a hard colour to describe, it is more the old-fashioned colour called 'lake'.
Rib Silver twist.

Hackle	Same colour as the body all the way up.
Shoulder	Blue jay.
Wings	As in No. 2, the golden pheasant perhaps predominating more.
Horns	Blue macaw.
Hooks	5–8

No. 5 The H.I.S.

This fly will be found noticed in the letter of a friend under 'Owenmore and Ballycroy' (see p. 50).

Tag	Silver tinsel.
Tail	A topping and some tippet.
Body	(no butt) Orange-yellow floss.
Rib	Gold tinsel.
Hackle	A coch-y-bonddu hackle.
Shoulder	A few turns of longish black heron. This gives it a spider-like look.
Wings	Brown mallard and two or three fibres of blue macaw, then a blue jay hackle over that.
Head	Black.
Hooks	5–8

A capital killer.

LOUGH MELVIN

This fine lough, some seven miles in length, contains salmon, grilse, charr, ferox, gillaroo, and other 'bastes' in abundance. Although it is not far from the Erne, the flies used are as sober as those of the Erne are often gaudy.

I also asked Rogan for a new pattern or two for Lough Melvin and he sent the following.

No. 1

Tag	Silver twist and orange floss.
Tail	A topping and sprigs of tippet and wood-duck with a small Indian crow feather.
Body	(no butt) Two-thirds a dirty yellowish olive pig's wool, one-third a dirty reddish claret which is tied on roughish.
Rib	Silver thread.
Hackle	None.
Shoulder	A claret hackle with a dirty dull orange one over it.
Wings	Two tippet feathers, a few sprigs of wood-duck and darkish mallard over.
Head	Black.
Hooks	7 or 8

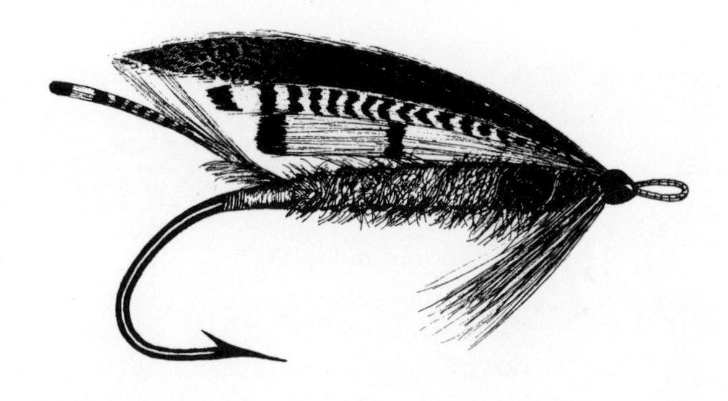

Mr Rogan's No. 1

No. 2

Tag	Silver twist and orange floss.
Tail	A topping and sprigs of wood-duck and tippet.
Body	(no butt) Dirty yellow olive pig's wool, a shade more yellow than No. 1.
Rib	Silver thread.
Hackle	The same colour as the body all the way up.
Shoulder	A dirty claret hackle.
Wings	Two tippet feathers with darkish mallard over.
Horns	Blue macaw.
Head	Black.
Hooks	7 or 8

No. 3

Tag	Silver twist and orange floss.
Tail	A topping.
Body	(no butt) Black pig's wool.

Rib Silver thread.
Hackle A black hackle all the way up, and running with it a dirty yellowish-red hackle which has one side stripped so as to be very sparse.
Shoulder A dirty claret hackle.
Wings Two tippet feathers (slightly larger than No. 2) with darkish mallard over and a sprig or two of dark wood-duck.
Head Black.
Hooks 7 or 8

The O'Donoghue *Colour plate 6*

This is a prime favourite which I got from the fishermen on the lough when fishing it several years ago.

Tag Gold tinsel and orange floss.
Tail A topping.
Butt Black ostrich herl.
Body Roughish, olive yellow pig's wool, merging into bright fiery claret, and that again into black.
Rib Gold twist.
Hackle Dark claret all the way up.
Shoulder Blue jay.
Wings Under wing, a tippet feather; brown mallard veiled over.
Horns Blue macaw.
Head Black.
Hooks 7 or 8

The Lough Gill Fly

LOUGH GILL

Another large lough near Sligo. There is a very favourite fly used here which sometimes kills on Lough Melvin; it is called:

The Lough Gill Fly

Tag Silver twist and orange floss.
Tail A topping and some mallard.
Body (no butt) Black mohair, with a broad ring of dark dirty red in the centre, also a few fibres of the same tied into the breast as a hackle.
Rib None.
Hackle See body.
Shoulder A blue jay hackle.
Wings A tippet feather and brown mallard wing.
Head Black.
Hook 9

THE MOY

The Moy is a large and rather open river which flows from Lough Conn, a very large lough. Above the weirs it resembles some of the streamy upper reaches of the Thames, where rush-beds abound. Much of the fishing, particularly below the weir, up to which the tide flows, is carried on from boats or cots. The opening of the weir has much improved the fishing in the upper reaches, but it has sadly deteriorated the angling below as the fish no longer rest there. It is a capital river for young hands to commence on as the work is easy, and the number of fish keep the attention fixed on the spot.

The Thunder and Lightning *Colour plate 6*

Tag Gold tinsel.
Tail A topping.
Butt Black ostrich herl.
Body Three turns of lightish orange floss, the rest of black floss.
Rib Gold tinsel.

Hackle A light orange hackle.
Shoulder A little blue jay.
Wings Dark brown mallard with a topping over it.
Horns Blue macaw.
Head Dark purple.
Hooks 7–10

The Orange and Grouse
Tag Silver tinsel
Tail A topping and a kingfisher feather.
Butt Black ostrich herl.
Body Three turns of lake floss and the rest of light orange floss.
Rib Silver tinsel.
Hackle Longest grouse which is trimmed on the breast, not the back; the grouse feather forming part of the wing.
Shoulder Blue jay, tied in sparely.
Wings Three or four toppings over the grouse feather.
Horns Blue macaw.
Head Black.
Hooks 10–12
This fly and the last are good general flies too.

We now have some Moy patterns without names.

No. 1
Tag Silver tinsel.
Tail A topping.
Butt None.
Body Two turns of buff floss, the rest of lake floss.
Rib Silver tinsel.
Hackle Medium orange.
Shoulder Blue jay.
Wings A tippet feather, then two spare cock of the rock feathers, fine strips of black partridge and golden pheasant tail; a topping over all.
Horns Blue macaw.
Head Purple.
Hooks 8–10

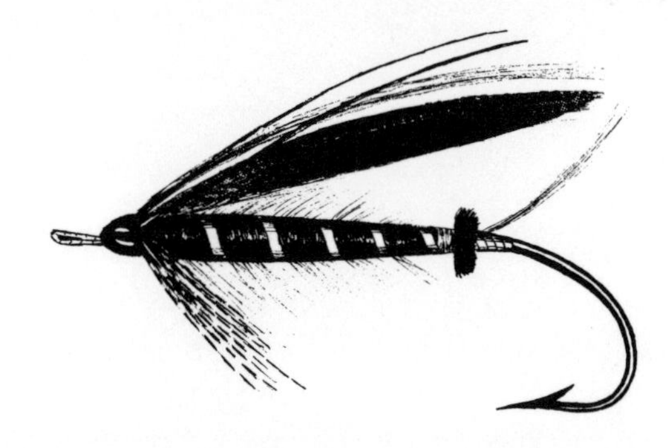

The Thunder and Lightning

No. 2
Tag Gold tinsel.
Tail A topping.
Butt Black ostrich herl.
Body Two turns of buff floss, the rest of copper-coloured floss.
Rib Gold tinsel.
Hackle A gallina hackle, trimmed on the breast but not on the back.
Shoulder A moderate amount of blue jay.
Wings Two or three thin cock of the rock hackles and reddish toucan feathers, sprigs of tippet and golden pheasant tail, brown mallard, and a topping over all.
Horns Blue macaw.
Head Purple.
Hooks 9 or 10

The above are standard flies and the sizes are chiefly for grilse. The opening of the weir has made a good deal of difference; for whereas formerly the best fishing was below the weir in moderately shallow water, very small flies were used. Now, however, the best fishing by far is higher up the river where the water is heavier and deeper and the flies are a size or two larger. I sent to Pat Hearns for some of the newer patterns with which we now continue.

No. 3

Tag	Silver tinsel.
Tail	A topping, some tippet, a kingfisher and a sprig or two of blue macaw.
Butt	Black ostrich herl.
Body	Two turns of orange floss, then dark blue, dark red, deep orange, and blue again, pig's wool.
Rib	Gold tinsel and gold twist.
Hackle	None.
Shoulder	A dark blue hackle with sprigs of tippet over, and one turn of jay over that.
Wings	Two tippet feathers, with two orange hackle points over, some golden pheasant tail over that, a bit of black partridge on either side and a topping over. A single kingfisher feather is tied in over the topping.
Head	Black.
Hooks	5–7

No. 4

Tag	Silver tinsel.
Tail	A topping, some tippet, and a kingfisher.
Butt	Black ostrich herl.
Body	Two turns of orange floss, the rest of dark reddish copper floss.
Rib	Silver tinsel and gold twist, side by side.
Hackle	Orange, three parts up.
Shoulder	Tippet sprigs with jay over.
Wings	Two tippet feathers, with two orange hackle points over, some golden pheasant tail over that, a bit of black partridge on either side and a topping over. A single kingfisher feather over the topping, as in No. 3.
Head	Black.
Hooks	5–7

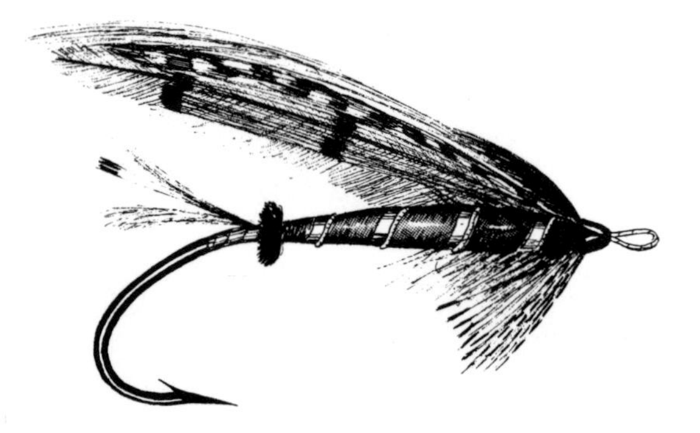

Pat Hearns' No. 4

No. 5

Of these larger patterns, No. 5 is our old friend the Thunder and Lightning mentioned above, only the hackle is a shade or two yellower. Hooks 5–7.

LOUGH CONN

These patterns are also from Hearns.

No. 1

Tag	Gold tinsel.
Tail	Some brown mallard and a few sprigs of tippet, and thin blue macaw.
Butt	None.
Body	Two turns of orange floss, the rest in three joints of rough pig's wool; dark blue, dark red, and deep orange.
Rib	Gold tinsel.
Hackle	Dark dirty green olive, over the orange only.
Shoulder	A grouse hackle.
Wings	Brown mallard.
Horns	Blue macaw.
Head	Black.
Hooks	8 or 9

No. 2

Tag	Gold tinsel.
Tail	A topping.
Butt	None.
Body	Two turns of orange floss, the rest of dark greenish olive pig's wool.

Rib Gold tinsel.
Hackle None.
Shoulder A brownish olive hackle with a dark blue one over it.
Wings Brown mallard with a topping over.
Horns Blue macaw.
Head Black.
Hooks 8 or 9

No. 3
Tag Gold tinsel.
Tail A topping.
Butt Black ostrich herl.
Body Two turns of orange floss, the rest of black floss.
Rib Gold tinsel.
Hackle A claret hackle all the way up.
Shoulder A darkish blue hackle.
Wings Two orange-yellow hackle points, small slips of brown mallard, golden pheasant tail, a little bit of argus pheasant, some sprigs of tippet, and a topping over all.
Horns Blue macaw.
Head Black.
Hooks 8 or 9

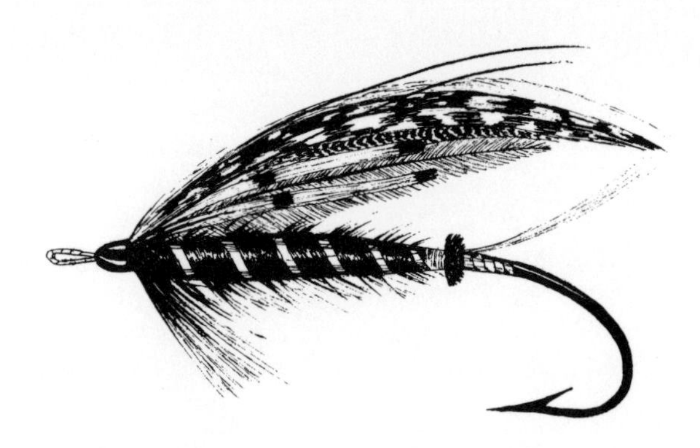

Pat Hearns' No. 3

THE OWENMORE AND BALLYCROY RIVERS

These two rivers run very near to each other. The Ballycroy is the river described by Maxwell in his *Wild Sports of the West.* Patterns again from Hearns.

The Owenmore *Colour plate 6*
This is one of the Erris flies which are curious specimens of art, and by no means easy to tie. They are very little used now and I give this dressing rather as a curiosity.
Tag Silver tinsel.
Tail A topping and a small jungle-cock.
Butt Black ostrich herl.
Body Five joints of yellow and black floss alternately. At each joint there are two turns of silver twist and one turn of a red hackle stained light olive. From the back of each joint, manes of mohair, the first darkish claret, second dark red, third darker claret, fourth darker red, and fifth a mixture of yellow, brown and red. Just under each mane as a support, is tied in a feather from the breast of an Indian crow, increasing in length (as do the manes) as they progress towards the head.
Rib and hackle See above – the turns at each joint.
Shoulder First an olive hackle, then the red rump feather of a golden pheasant tied in as a hackle, over that again a turn or two of blue jay.
Wings Tippet fibres, golden pheasant tail and brown mallard followed by a topping.
Horns Blue macaw.
Head Black.
Hooks 8 or 9

Next is another fly with joints and manes, and which has no name.
Tag Silver twist.
Tail A topping.
Butt One turn of orange floss.

Body	Five joints each of black floss. At each joint, two turns of fine silver thread, except for the three lowest joints which have one turn of orange floss above the silver thread. The two lowest manes are a dirty clarety red, the next two are a mixture of yellow, olive, and light claret. The manes are again of mohair increasing in length as they progress towards the head.
Shoulder	A brown olive hackle with a little blue jay over it.
Wings	A slip of tippet, and over it slips of mallard and peacock.
Horns	Blue macaw.
Head	Black.
Hooks	6–10 and sea trout size in summer.

There are a great variety of these jointed bodies used in Erris; some have blue and yellow, or blue, yellow, and black joints alternately, with black or coloured herls or hackles at each joint. They are considered indispensable enchantments by those who admire them, and as they are a peculiar class of fly, I have gone into them, though my own faith is by no means implicit. My friend Mr S. and his cousin rented the Ballycroy river for some years, and I wrote to him for a cast from his experience, as, although I fished the Owenmore several times, I only fished the Ballycroy once. Herewith I give his letter to me from which it will be seen that he has no faith whatever in the jointed and maned flies which are supposed to emanate from and flourish particularly in Erris.

Dear F. The flies on the Owenmore and Owenduff rivers some years ago were always what is called 'jointed', and were made in two ways; the first had the joints made of hackles of divers colours, tied as in the pattern I send you, but of course on a smaller hook. The enclosed is a specimen from the Dee, in Aberdeen, to which river it was transported by Mr Gordon, from Ballycroy and has since been naturalised. The other jointed fly is made thus: topping for tail, then three different colours of floss silk for body, with three rings of twist at the end of each, and standing out from these joints three long manes of different coloured mohair, ordinary mixed wing, and hackle at shoulder. It is a very difficult fly to tie, and not worth a rush when tied, except that is in its *dry* state it looks very pretty; when in the water, on the contrary, it all bags together, and I never did much good with it. The fly on the contrary, with the plain turkey wing was an invention of our own, and killed 48 salmon and 137 white trout in one week on the Owenduff. The fly with the mallard wing and fiery body also kills right well on both rivers, and so do the Ballina flies, more especially one of Pat Hearns' called the Thunder and Lightning. An equally great pet is the enclosed, with the frayed gut. He is confoundedly ugly sir, having been composed by your humble servant; but treat him with respect, for this very year that identical specimen has slain six *Salmo salar* in the river Erne that thou knowest of. I enclose four or five more of what MacGowan calls his Ballycroy flies, but they are awful imposters (on second thought I don't, for they are no use at all). The fish, in fact, like plain sober mallard and turkey, and furnace hackles, with either orange or brown bodies, and jay about the shoulders.

H.I.S.

I never could understand how the Nicholson, a regular Erris notion, formerly got on the Tay, but the course of its introduction becomes pretty clear from the above. The fly referred to strongly resembles the Nicholson. However, here is the pattern (also illustrated) that killed the 48 salmon and 137 white trout in a week. I should tell you that the white trout at Ballycroy run up to six or seven pounds weight and average from two to three pounds.

Tag	Gold thread.
Tail	A slip of mottled brown turkey and a tuft of orange mohair.
Butt	Black ostrich herl.
Body	Half orange mohair (inclining to darkish) and half black mohair.
Rib	Gold thread over the orange mohair and gold tinsel over the black.

Hackle Black over black mohair only, ending on the shoulder.
Shoulder See hackle.
Wings Rich brown mottled turkey.
Head Black.
Hooks 9 or 10

Here is another pattern from Mr S.
Tag Silver thread and orange floss.
Tail A topping.
Butt None.
Body Two-fifths dark dirty orange-yellow pig's wool, three-fifths darkish claret pig's wool.
Rib Broad gold tinsel.
Shoulder (No body hackle.) A medium claret hackle with blue jay over.
Wings Brown mallard.
Head Black.
Hooks 9 or 10

Before we move on I will include one more pattern from Hearns.
Tag Silver tinsel.
Tail A small topping, a slip of black partridge, a kingfisher, and an Indian crow breast feather.
Butt Black ostrich herl.
Body Three turns of orange floss, the rest of black floss.
Rib Silver tinsel.
Hackle Gallina stained yellow, clipped at the breast, not on the back.
Shoulder A tippet feather tied in as a hackle with blue jay over.
Wings A red hackle and a yellow hackle, a red rump feather from a golden pheasant, sprigs of tippet, slips of golden pheasant tail and peacock, and a large blue chatterer feather (or a kingfisher) over.
Cheeks Indian crow.
Horns Blue macaw.
Head Black.
Hooks 6–10
This fly can be varied by using lake floss instead of black.

GALWAY AND CONNEMARA
(Costello, Ballynahinch, & Co.)

The Costello I do not know from experience, but the Doohullah rivers and loughs I have fished. The Ballynahinch river is short and not very large, but what there is of it above the weir is pretty. The lakes, for scenery – particularly the upper lake, Lough Inagh – are lovely, and the sport at times is good, more particularly with white trout, and a good take of salmon may be got at times, wind, weather, and water permitting.
These patterns were sent to me by Mr Nicholson of Galway. Some are old acquaintances renewed.

No. 1
Tag Gold tinsel and orange floss.
Tail A topping.
Butt None.
Body Silver grey wool or fur. (A regular River Lee body.)
Rib Silver twist.
Hackle A cuckoo dun hackle to match the body.
Shoulder Blue jay.
Wings A long tippet nearly the full length of the body, some peacock and a few sprigs of green peacock herl, then red, blue, and yellow macaw sprigs – the red most plentiful.
Head Black.
Hooks 7–11

No. 2
Tag Gold tinsel and orange floss.
Tail Gallina.
Butt None.
Body Two-thirds medium blue floss, the upper third medium orange floss.
Rib Silver tinsel.
Hackle Bright brown olive.
Shoulder Blue jay.
Wings Golden pheasant tail, cock pheasant tail (from the more common breed), peacock and gallina.
Horns Blue macaw.
Head Black.
Hooks 7–11

No. 3

Tag	Gold tinsel.
Tail	A topping.
Butt	Black ostrich herl.
Body	Three-fifths medium orange floss, the upper two-fifths darkish blue floss.
Rib	Gold tinsel.
Hackle	A darkish claret hackle over the blue, ending on the shoulder.
Wings	A largish tippet feather, brown speckled turkey, golden pheasant tail, blue, green, and yellow swan.
Horns	Blue macaw.
Head	Black.
Hooks	7–11

No. 4

This is a weird-looking fly: the contrast between the dark blue body and light yellow hackle is so strong.

Tag	Gold tinsel and light orange floss.
Tail	A topping.
Butt	None.
Body	Dark blue floss.
Rib	Silver tinsel.
Hackle	Light yellow.
Shoulder	Blue jay.
Wings	Brown mallard, golden pheasant tail (streaked), and some peacock sword feather herls.
Horns	Blue macaw.
Hooks	7–11

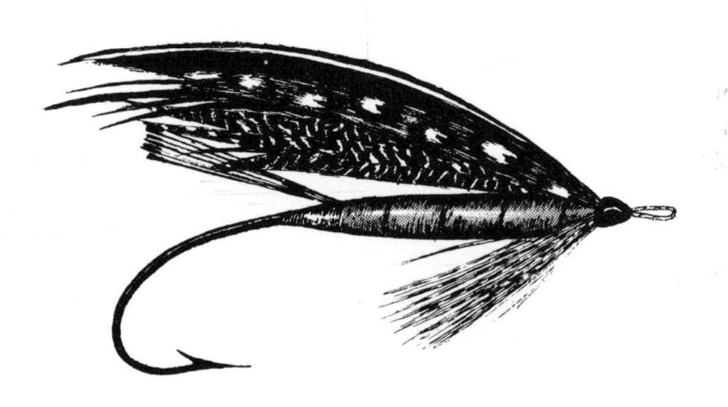

Mr Macredy's Fly

No. 5

Tag	Gold twist and yellow floss.
Tail	Teal, mallard, green parrot, and flamingo.
Butt	Black ostrich herl.
Body	Two-thirds ruby floss and one-third medium blue floss.
Rib	None.
Hackle	A flamingo feather is tied in at the breast and at the shoulder as a hackle; the part on the breast is clipped.
Shoulder	See hackle.
Wings	A red rump feather from a golden pheasant, light yellow-green parrot, a little pintail and brown mallard over all.
Horns	Blue macaw.
Hooks	7–11

No. 6

Tag	Silver thread and light blue floss.
Tail	A topping.
Butt	Black ostrich herl.
Body	Light orange floss.
Rib	Silver thread.
Hackle	A black hackle all the way up.
Shoulder	Blue jay.
Wings	Mottled argus pheasant, sprigs of tippet, green parrot, and golden pheasant tail.
Head	Black.
Hooks	7–11

Mr Macredy of Lisoughter Lodge has sent me a new fly for these waters and it is a very nice one.

Tag	Gold thread and orange floss.
Tail	Tippet sprigs.
Body	(no butt) Very dark brown floss with a red tinge when held up to the light – dark fiery brown perhaps.
Rib	Gold thread.
Shoulder	(No body hackle.) Blue jay.
Wings	Fibres of bustard (plentiful), gallina, golden pheasant tail, violet, pink, and yellow swan.
Head	Black.
Hooks	9–11

LOUGH INCHIQUIN

The Inchiquin

This fly is used chiefly on Lough Inchiquin, but it is a standard pattern throughout the west of Ireland; it has no tag, butt, or body hackle.

Tail Brown mallard and some purple fibres from a peacock's breast.
Body Fiery red pig's wool.
Rib Gold thread.
Shoulder A natural red cock's hackle.
Wings Mallard with fibres from a peacock's breast over.
Head Black.
Hooks 10 or 11

The Inchiquin

THE LENNAN AND LOUGH FERN IN DONEGAL

The Lennan is a dull river and not much use for salmon fishing; but Lough Fern from which it runs gives fair sport at times. Lough Fern is not a large water; it is also weedy and shallow and hardly worth going to unless the angler chances to be going to or from Gweedore, *via* Rathmelton.

The Inchiquin fly does well there, and will do better if, instead of a mallard and peacock-breast wing, plain brown turkey or golden pheasant tail are used. The body and hackle can also be varied by being made more or less sandy. The fly should be rough and well picked out. Hooks, 8–10.

THE SHANNON

The Shannon is a very large and heavy river. The water in places is very rapid, broken, and dangerous to the angler's hopes, as it often occurs that the place where a fish is hooked is so infested with hidden and awkward rocks that the angler is obliged to hold on and not to give a yard of line if he can avoid it. At Castle Connell the river has long been celebrated as a first-class sporting water which frequently offers magnificent salmon fishing. At Killaloe the water is more open and easy to fish. Lough Derg, an expansion of the Shannon, gives splendid fishing for large trout, and when the fish are in the humour great numbers are taken with the cross line. As on the Moy, much of the fishing is done from cots.

The large heavy water Shannon flies are very showy affairs. Here is one which was dressed for me by my friend Mr Blacker, years ago. It is quite a work of art.

The Shannon *Colour plate 6*

Tag Gold tinsel and lemon-yellow floss.
Tail Two toppings, scarlet ibis and blue macaw.
Butt Black ostrich herl.
Body Of floss silk in four joints, pale blue, orange, puce, and pea green. Above each joint is a turn of ostrich herl of the same colour and over each herl a hackle, also of the same colour.
Rib A turn of gold thread below each joint.
Hackle See body.
Shoulder One or two golden pheasant rump feathers as hackles.

Wings	Two bright yellow macaw feathers with a black streak down the centre, a strip of dark-speckled argus pheasant and sprigs of tippet on either side, and three large toppings over all.
Cheeks	Two or three slips of ibis on either side and over them a small feather of purple lory (a small Polynesian parrot) or any small purple feather.
Horns	Blue macaw.
Head	Black.
Hook	2

I do not think the jointed body by any means necessary, nor is it used generally on the Shannon. The wing given is, I know, pretty much used when the feathers can be obtained, but the yellow macaw feathers of the right size are not easy to obtain, and make the fly expensive to dress. Probably an orange body would answer all requisites as orange is in favour on the Shannon.

My good friend Mr Nicholay, well known among anglers, for many years rented a capital stretch of the Castle Connell water. He is quite a connoisseur in flies, and has sent me of late some flies which are very beautiful creatures. Here they are:

No. 1

Tag	Silver tinsel.
Tail	A long Indian crow feather and a topping.
Butt	Red ostrich herl.
Body	Silver tinsel.
Rib	Gold thread.
Hackle	Dark blue all the way up.
Shoulder	A yellow hackle from an Indian crow with a palish green macaw hackle over it.
Wings	Sprigs of blue and red macaw, orange and yellow swan, gallina, and golden pheasant tail.
Cheeks	Longish kingfisher.
Head	Red ostrich herl.
Hook	4, but the length of a No. 7 only.

No. 2

Tag	Silver tinsel and darkish blue floss.
Butt	Black ostrich herl.
Tail	A medium-sized Indian crow and a topping.
Body	Yellowish orange floss.
Rib	Gold tinsel.
Hackle	A light pea-green parrot clipped on the breast but left long on the shoulder, and on the back to form part of the wings.
Shoulder	See hackle.
Wings	(Including the hackle.) Two long Indian crow feathers (the under one the longest), a few sprigs of golden pheasant tail, gallina, blue macaw, and yellow swan.
Cheeks	A pair of smaller Indian crow feathers on either side standing up and out.
Head	Black.
Hook	4, but the length of a No. 7 only.

No. 3

Tag	Gold tinsel and golden floss.
Tail	An Indian crow and a topping.
Butt	None.
Body	Dark blue floss.
Rib	Gold tinsel and gold twist side by side.
Hackle	Dark blue all the way up.
Shoulder	Blue jay.
Wings	Two or three deep orange (almost crimson) hackles; outside them a pale powder blue macaw feather on one side, and an orange-red one on the other. Two or three large toppings over followed by sprigs of golden pheasant tail, bustard, wood-duck, and red macaw.
Cheeks	Indian crow.
Head	A large head of lemon crewel.
Hook	4 normal size.

No. 4

Tag	Gold thread and pea-green floss.
Tail	Indian crow and Himalayan pheasant hackle. (This feather is like a red dyed topping.)
Body	(no butt) Two turns of thick orange floss, the rest dark blue floss.

Rib	Broad gold tinsel and gold thread together.
Hackle	A dark blue hackle with a yellow Indian crow feather, all the way up.
Shoulder	Blue jay.
Wings	One long bright yellow macaw feather, with an orange-red one on either side; over that six or seven toppings followed by sprigs of bustard, golden pheasant tail, red and blue macaw.
Head	A large head of yellow crewel.
Hook	This fly is dressed on a No. 6 double hook.

No. 5

The last was a gay fellow, but this is more brilliant still.

Tag	Silver tinsel and pea-green floss.
Tail	Himalayan pheasant hackle (or a topping dyed red).
Body	(no butt) Medium orange floss.
Rib	Silver tinsel and gold thread together.
Hackle	Powder blue macaw all the way up and ending on shoulder.
Shoulder	See above.
Wings	One long bright yellow macaw feather, with an orange-red one on either side; over that six or seven toppings followed by sprigs of bustard, golden pheasant tail, red and blue macaw. (Same as No. 4.)
Cheeks	Large blue chatterer feathers or kingfisher.
Head	A large head of crewel the same colour as the cheeks.
Hook	6 double, as before.

KILLARNEY AND THE FLESK

The far-famed lakes of Killarney often hold a good many salmon but the nets and cross lines make single rod fishing rather a precarious sport. The Flesk which runs into the head of the lakes is a pretty little river but needs water to give sport. A day or two's rain, however, brings the fish up out of the lakes and some good sport can be expected, but it runs off just as quickly as it rises. Fish run into the lakes very early.

Here are some good patterns for the lakes and the Flesk.

No. 1

Tag	Silver tinsel.
Tail	Some tippet and a kingfisher feather.
Butt	Black ostrich herl.
Body	Darkish medium blue floss.
Rib	None.
Hackle	Blue jay all the way up.
Shoulder	An orange hackle.
Wings	Brown turkey.
Horns	Blue macaw.
Head	Black.
Hooks	6–8

No. 2

Tag	Silver twist.
Tail	A topping with some mallard and a kingfisher feather.
Butt	Red wool.

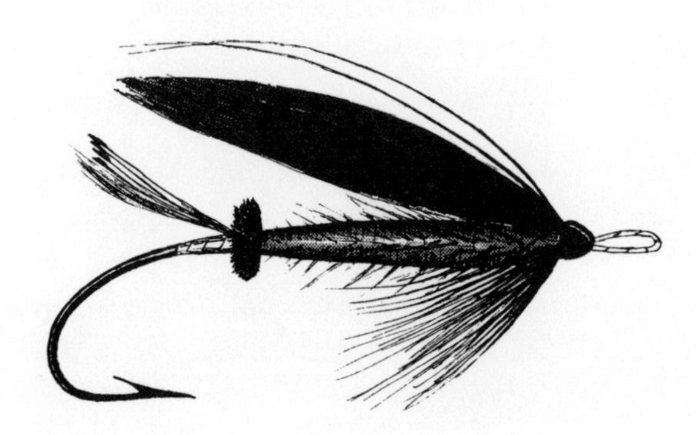

No. 1 for Killarney and the Flesk

Body Darkish medium blue floss.
Rib Gold tinsel.
Hackle Blue jay all the way up.
Shoulder Orange hackle.
Wings Brown turkey.
Horns Blue macaw.
Head Black.
Hooks 6–8

No. 3

Tag Ruby silk floss.
Tail Mallard and tippet.
Butt Black ostrich herl.
Body Pale olive-green floss.
Rib Gold tinsel.
Hackle Medium blue.
Shoulder A brown olive hackle.
Wings A mixed wing of brown turkey, argus, and golden pheasant tail.
Head Blue ostrich herl.
Hooks 6–8

No. 4

Tag Gold tinsel and lemon-yellow wool.
Tail A topping with a kingfisher feather and fibres of mallard and gallina.
Butt None.
Body Copper-coloured mohair.
Rib None.
Hackle Medium blue ending on the shoulder.
Wings Married slices of brown turkey and golden pheasant tail, and some fibres of blue macaw.
Head Black.
Hooks 6–8

The bodies for these four flies should be sparely dressed.

THE LAUNE

The salmon enter Killarney through the Laune; a fine wide river. It is rather heavy down towards Killorglin, but streamy and likely in the upper reaches. In the early part of the season the fish do not rest long and make at once for the lakes. Later on, however, good sport may be had in it.

The bodies for all the Laune flies must be dressed as spare as possible, the hackles are short in the fibre, and of the same size as the Killarney and Flesk flies. A peculiarity of the fishermen in this part of the world is that they use a hook some two sizes larger in the bend than would commonly be used for the same fly, breaking off a piece of the shank to get the fly to the right size.

The flies for Killarney, the Flesk, and the Laune were tied for me by the local anglers there when I was fishing in that quarter some years ago.

No. 1 *Colour plate 6*

Tag Orange floss.
Tail Tippet sprigs.
Butt Black ostrich herl.
Body Half bright medium green, and half light orange floss.
Rib Narrow gold tinsel.
Hackle Medium blue.
Shoulder A brown hackle, not too long in the fibre.
Wings Brown turkey with a few fibres of tippet and blue macaw thrown in.
Head Black.
Hooks 6–8, slightly shorter in the shank than normal. The same for the following two flies.

No. 2

Tag Orange floss.
Tail Tippet sprigs and a topping.
Butt Black ostrich herl.
Body In four joints; ruby-red, orange, ruby-red, orange. Each of floss.
Rib Narrow gold tinsel.
Hackle Blue jay.
Shoulder A short brown hackle.

Wings	Brown turkey with a few fibres of tippet and blue macaw thrown in. (As in No. 1.)
Head	Black.
Hooks	6–8 (short)

No. 3

Tag	Silver tinsel.
Tail	Tippet sprigs and a kingfisher feather.
Butt	Black ostrich herl.
Body	Medium orange floss.
Rib	Narrow gold tinsel.
Hackle	A grouse hackle clipped short all round.
Shoulder	A light orange hackle.
Wings	A tippet feather, golden pheasant tail, and a small portion of golden pheasant tail stained claret.
Head	Black.
Hooks	6–8 (short)

THE LEE, CORK

In some parts the Lee is rather a quiet and placid river, but in many places it breaks out into fine bold pools and streams which form the very beau-ideal of the angler. It is a fine spring river which has been well looked after of late years by the Cork club.

The Yellow Anthony

Tag	Silver twist.
Tail	A topping.
Butt	A scrap of yellow mohair.
Body	Bluish silver-grey wool or fur.
Rib	Fine silver twist.
Hackle	A silver-grey dun hackle.
Shoulder	A dirty-yellow hackle.
Wings	A little peacock with mallard over it.
Horns	Blue macaw.
Head	Black.
Hooks	6–9

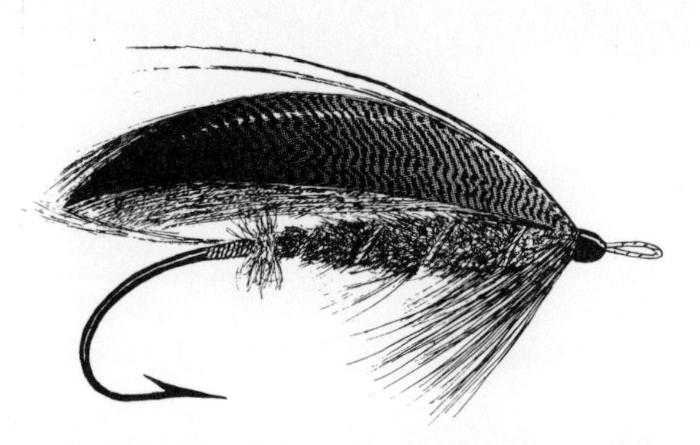

The Yellow Anthony

The Orange Anthony

Tag	Silver twist.
Tail	A topping.
Butt	A scrap of orange mohair.
Body	Three turns of darkish blue mohair, the rest of silver-grey wool or fur.
Rib	Fine silver twist.
Hackle	A darkish blue hackle over the blue part, and a silver-grey cuckoo dun hackle over the silver-grey part.
Shoulder	A medium orange hackle.
Wings	A little peacock, with mallard veiled over.
Cheeks	Kingfisher.
Horns	Blue macaw.
Head	Black.
Hooks	6–9

Mr Haynes sent me six flies which are good for the Lee and the Blackwater.

No. 1

Tag	Silver tinsel and orange floss.
Tail	Tippet and gallina.
Butt	None.
Body	In short joints of wool – dark blue, orange-red (getting to vermilion), darkish green (inclining to sage green), and silver-grey.

Hackle	Hackles of each colour to match the joints of the body.
Shoulder	Orange-red.
Wings	Sprigs of common cock pheasant; yellow, blue, and red swan, and brown mallard veiled over.
Horns	Blue macaw.
Head	Black.
Hooks	6–9

No. 2

Tag	Silver tinsel and orange floss.
Tail	Tippet and wood-duck.
Butt	Black ostrich herl.
Body	Two-fifths darkish medium blue floss, then three-fifths silver-grey fur.
Rib	Fine silver tinsel over the blue joint, then narrow silver tinsel over the silver-grey fur.
Hackle	A blue hackle of the same shade over the blue joint, a yellow hackle at the joint, and a hackle of the same shade over the silver-grey fur.
Shoulder	A claret hackle.
Wings	Red parrot, wood-duck, and brown mallard.
Horns	Blue macaw.
Head	Black.
Hooks	6–9

No. 3

Tag	Silver tinsel and orange floss.
Tail	A topping.
Butt	None.
Body	Bright medium blue chenille.
Rib	Silver tinsel.
Hackle	A yellow hackle with the slightest tinge of orange, all the way up.
Shoulder	Jay.
Wings	Sprigs of tippet, a bit of golden pheasant rump feather, a little florican bustard, gallina and brown mallard.
Horns	Blue macaw.
Hooks	6–9

No. 4

Tag	Silver tinsel and dark blue floss.
Tail	A topping.
Butt	Black ostrich herl.
Body	Black floss.
Rib	Silver tinsel.
Hackle	A yellow hackle with the slightest tinge of orange, all the way up.
Shoulder	Jay.
Wings	Sprigs of tippet, a bit of golden pheasant rump feather, a little florican bustard, gallina and brown mallard (as before).
Horns	Blue macaw.
Hooks	6–9

Now comes two fancies.

No. 5

Tag	Silver tinsel and orange floss.
Tail	A topping.
Butt	Black ostrich herl.
Body	Dark blue floss.
Rib	Silver thread.
Hackle	Dark claret all the way up.
Shoulder	Jay.
Wings	Made of six hackle points, two scarlet in the middle, violet on either side of them, and clear yellow outside.
Head	Black.
Hooks	6–9

No. 6

I call this fly the Spider.

Tag	Silver tinsel and dark blue floss.
Tail	Two small jungle-cock eye feathers.
Butt	None.
Body	Two turns of black floss, the rest of light orange.
Rib	Silver tinsel.
Hackle	A large blue heron hackle all the way up the body and flowing back from the head to a point about half an inch longer than the hook.
Shoulder	A short black hackle dressed as a ruff.

Wings	A pair of jungle-cock feathers reaching to the tag and lying alongside the hook to hide the body.
Head	Black.
Hooks	6–9

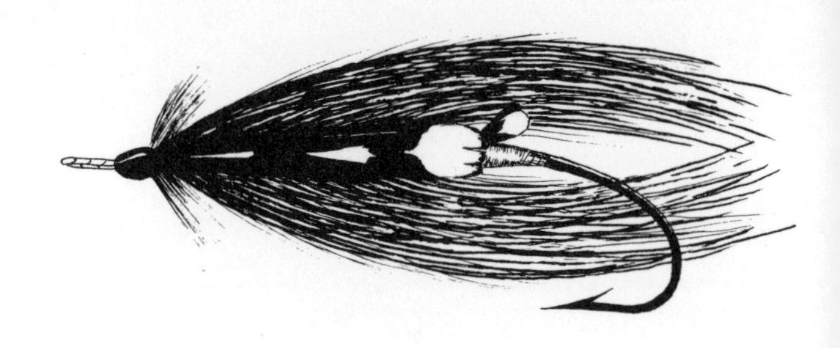

No. 6 (The Spider)

THE CORK BLACKWATER

The following three flies I got with others from Mr Haynes of Patrick Street, Cork.

No. 1

Tag	Silver tinsel and orange floss.
Tail	Black partridge, tippet and mallard sprigs.
Butt	Black ostrich herl.
Body	Silver-grey fur (same as in the Lee flies) for one-third of the body, the rest of medium yellowish-green mohair.
Rib	Narrow gold tinsel.
Hackle	A silver-grey cuckoo dun hackle (clipped) over the silver-grey fur, and a green hackle of the same shade over the mohair.
Shoulder	An orange hackle.
Wings	Slips from the streaked feather of a golden pheasant tail, brown mallard over, sprigs of red and green parrot.
Horns	Blue macaw.
Head	Black.
Hooks	6–8

No. 2

Tag	Gold tinsel.
Tail	A topping and some tippet.
Butt	Black ostrich herl.
Body	In three equal parts; darkish blue, claret, and grey fur.
Hackle	Blue, claret, and grey hackles to match the body joints; the lower (blue) hackle is clipped.
Shoulder	A yellow hackle.
Wings	Sprigs of bustard, brown turkey, tippet, green parrot, and brown mallard veiled over.
Head	Black.
Hooks	6–8

No. 3

Tag	Silver tinsel and orange floss.
Tail	Sprigs of tippet, mallard, green mohair, and gallina stained pale blue.
Butt	None.
Body	Apple-green floss.
Rib	Fine gold twist.
Hackle	Blue jay all the way up.
Shoulder	An orange hackle.
Wings	Golden pheasant tail (streaked), bustard, green parrot, and brown mallard veiled over.

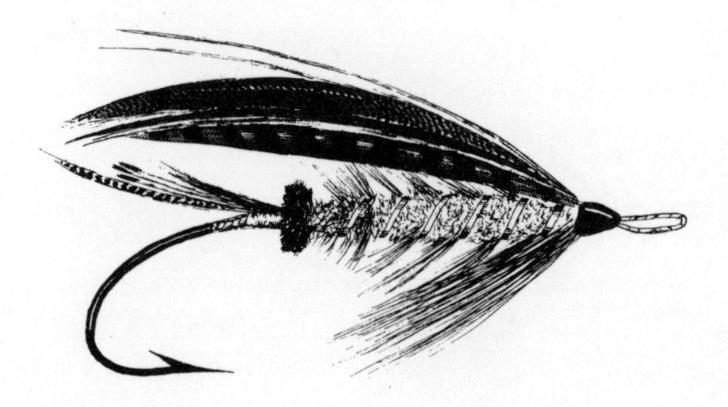

Mr Haynes' No. 1

Head	Black.
Hooks	6–8

These flies may be dressed smaller for the summer. Add to these the patterns for the Lee.

THE BANDON

The Bandon is a pretty river which produces a good many salmon. Patterns again from Mr Haynes.

No. 1

Tag	Silver tinsel and orange floss.
Tail	A topping.
Butt	None.
Body	Black chenille.
Rib	Silver tinsel.
Hackle	Claret all the way up.
Shoulder	Blue jay.
Wings	A bunch of tippet sprigs and brown mallard.
Horns	Blue macaw.
Hooks	7 or 8

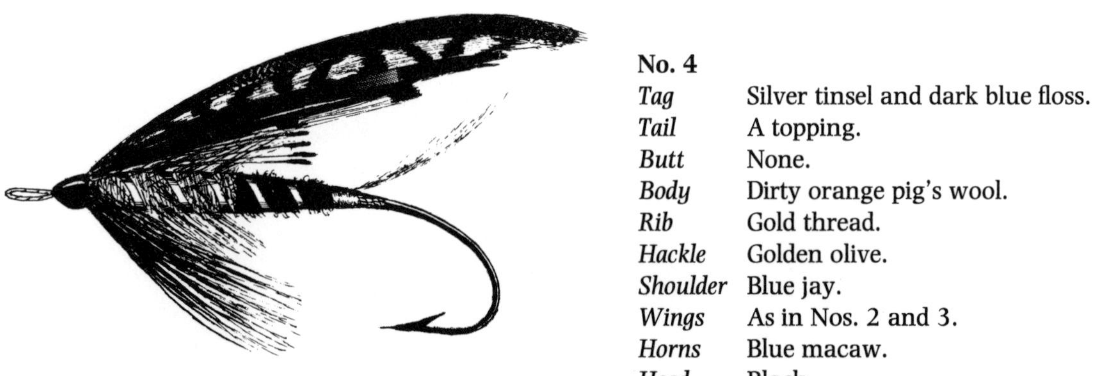

Mr Haynes' No. 2

No. 2

Tag	Silver tinsel and orange floss.
Tail	A topping.
Butt	None.
Body	Lower half, rough dirty-orange wool; upper half, dark silver-grey wool.
Rib	Silver tinsel.
Hackle	A cuckoo dun hackle over the silver-grey wool.
Shoulder	A darkish blue hackle.
Wings	A slice of ibis or red parrot, tippet sprigs, florican bustard, golden pheasant tail, and brown mallard.
Horns	Blue macaw.
Head	Black.
Hooks	7 or 8

No. 3

Tag	Silver tinsel and bright yellow wool.
Tail	A topping.
Butt	None.
Body	Medium blue wool.
Rib	Silver tinsel.
Hackle	The same shade of blue as the body.
Shoulder	Bright yellow.
Wings	A slice of ibis or red parrot, tippet sprigs, florican bustard, golden pheasant tail, and brown mallard (as in No. 2).
Horns	Blue macaw.
Head	Black.
Hooks	7 or 8

No. 4

Tag	Silver tinsel and dark blue floss.
Tail	A topping.
Butt	None.
Body	Dirty orange pig's wool.
Rib	Gold thread.
Hackle	Golden olive.
Shoulder	Blue jay.
Wings	As in Nos. 2 and 3.
Horns	Blue macaw.
Head	Black.
Hooks	7 or 8

No. 5

Tag	Silver tinsel and orange floss.
Tail	A topping and some tippet.
Butt	None.
Body	Two turns of dark blue floss and one turn of orange floss; the rest of dark silver-grey fur.
Rib	Silver tinsel.
Hackle	A cuckoo dun hackle over the silver-grey fur.
Shoulder	A vermilion-red hackle with a slight orange tinge.
Wings	A slice of ibis or red parrot, tippet sprigs, florican bustard, and brown mallard (as before without the golden pheasant tail).
Horns	Blue macaw.
Head	Black.
Hooks	7 or 8

No. 6

Tag	Silver tinsel.
Tail	A topping.
Butt	Emerald peacock herl.
Body	Medium orange floss.
Rib	Silver thread.
Hackle	A grizzled silver-grey hackle all the way up.
Shoulder	Blue jay.
Wings	As in No. 5.
Horns	Blue macaw.
Head	Black.
Hooks	7 or 8

THE CARAGH AND LOUGH CURRANE

The Caragh is a short river which in the upper part is rather dull and heavy; in the lower part, however, there are some good pools and streams. It yields fair sport, but would give very fine sport if the fish had but fair play; but what with the weir, the nets, and the crosslines, they are woefully harried, and beyond this the alteration in the netting season of late years takes most of the few fish left. Lough Currane is a fine sheet of water.

The same flies kill both on Lough Currane and the Caragh, and for the most part they are much the same as those for the Lee and Blackwater; greys, blues and clarets running more or less through them.

Patterns again from Mr Haynes.

No. 1

Tag	Gold tinsel and orange floss.
Tail	A topping.
Butt	None.
Body	Lower half, dark blue wool; upper half, dark claret wool.
Rib	Fine gold twist.
Hackle	A dark blue hackle over the lower half, and a dark claret one over the upper half, each of the same shade as the wool.
Shoulder	Gallina stained pale blue.
Wings	Golden pheasant tail (streaked), some tippet, and brown mallard veiled over.
Cheeks	Kingfisher.
Head	Black.
Hooks	7 or 8

No. 2

Tag	Silver tinsel and orange floss.
Tail	Tippet and mallard.
Butt	None.
Body	Dark blue mohair.
Rib	Silver twist.
Hackle	Very dark blue.
Shoulder	Blue jay.
Wings	Tippet, peacock, red parrot, and brown mallard veiled over.
Head	Black.
Hooks	10 or 11

No. 3

Tag	Silver tinsel and orange floss.
Tail	Tippet and brown mallard.
Butt	None.
Body	Dirty dark brown olive wool.
Rib	Fine gold twist.
Hackle	The same shade as the body.
Shoulder	A light orange hackle.
Wings	Tippet, florican bustard, and brown mallard veiled over.
Horns	Blue macaw.
Head	Black.
Hooks	10 or 11

Mr Haynes' No. 3

No. 4

Tag	Silver tinsel and orange floss.
Tail	Tippet, a topping, green parrot and mallard.
Butt	None.
Body	Dirty olive-yellow pig's wool.
Rib	Gold twist.
Hackle	Medium blue.
Shoulder	A light orange hackle.
Wings	Tippet, golden pheasant tail, green parrot, and brown mallard veiled over.
Head	Black.
Hooks	8 or 9

Years ago I had this pattern from Blacker and after keeping it twenty years ineffective, I killed three fish with it on the Tay before the loop broke.

THE KERRY BLACKWATER

The same character of flies prevails here.

No. 1

Tag	Gold tinsel.
Tail	A topping and some tippet.
Butt	Black ostrich herl.
Body	In three joints, darkish blue, silver-grey, and claret fur.
Rib	Narrow gold tinsel.
Hackle	Three hackles, blue, grey, and claret to match the body joints; the lower (blue) hackle is clipped.
Shoulder	A yellow hackle with blue jay over it.
Wings	Tippet, hen pheasant, red, and green parrot, and brown mallard veiled over.
Head	Black.
Hooks	7–11

No. 2

Tag	Silver tinsel.
Tail	Mallard, tippet, and lavender macaw.
Butt	Black ostrich herl.
Body	Medium orange floss.
Rib	Fine gold thread.
Hackle	Greenish-olive.
Shoulder	Blue jay.
Wings	Tippet and mallard.
Horns	Blue macaw.
Head	Black.
Hooks	7–11

No. 3

Tag	Fine gold twist.
Tail	A topping.
Butt	A turn of scarlet crewel.
Body	Two-thirds dark blue floss, the upper third of orange floss.
Rib	Silver tinsel.
Hackle	Blue jay.
Shoulder	Orange hackle.
Wings	Tippet and mallard.
Horns	Blue macaw.
Head	Black.
Hooks	7–11

THE SUIR

To obtain patterns for the Suir and Nore, I wrote to Mr Brady and he most kindly forwarded me the following patterns with a note from a resident on the river – Mr Staples – an extract from which note I append.

I have not fished either Nore or Suir for two years. There has not been a fish up the Nore past Kilkenny this year, after all our trouble and expense, owing to the perfect system of poaching established on that unfortunate river; I have, therefore, only a few old patterns to send you. The two flies marked '*My own pattern*, best kind', I found to beat every other fly on the Suir, tied to suit the water, large or small, and with the silk body either blue with purple hackle, or yellow or dark orange, over dark purple or dark mauve-coloured silk; in this manner it can be varied to suit any taste; you must use argus pheasant hackle round the shoulders. Both these flies are tied by myself, and have killed many fish.
The little grey fly is also famous on the Suir, and the other flies I have found very good on the Nore.

Here are Mr Staples' patterns:

No. 1

Tag	Silver tinsel and orange-yellow floss.
Tail	Sprigs of bustard and ibis.
Butt	Black ostrich herl.
Body	Red plum-coloured floss.
Rib	Silver twist.
Hackle	Light orange.
Shoulder	Argus pheasant hackle.
Wings	A good bunch of *green* peacock herl, with strips of brown turkey with dun points mixed, and a topping over all.
Head	Black.
Hook	5

No. 2

Tag	Silver tinsel and lemon floss.
Tail	A topping.
Butt	Black ostrich herl.
Body	Red rum-coloured floss.
Rib	Silver twist.
Hackle	Light orange.
Shoulder	Argus pheasant hackle (from the breast of the bird).
Wings	Under wing, a small tippet feather. Over wing, a little *green* peacock, some brown mallard, and a strand or two of gallina and grey mallard stained yellow.
Horns	Blue macaw.
Head	Black.
Hook	10

No. 3

This is the grey fly referred to in the letter; it is not much bigger than a trout fly.

Tag	Silver tinsel.
Tail	A topping.
Butt	Black ostrich herl.
Body	A turn of orange floss, the rest silver grey fur.
Rib	Silver twist.
Hackle	None.
Shoulder	A very pale yellow hackle.
Wings	A few sprigs of small tippet, brown mallard over it, and yellow stained gallina over that. The wings should be rather thin.
Head	Black.
Hooks	10–12

In the season of 1879 I met a gentleman who with one or two friends rents a fine stretch of the Suir, and who fishes it habitually; he very kindly promised to send me some patterns from the Suir – which he did in March 1880. The flies sent are of the largest spring size tied on hooks from No. 2 downwards; and no doubt they are used in heavy and rough water. I give you these patterns:

The Mystery

Tag	Silver twist and orange floss.
Tail	A topping and an Indian crow.
Butt	Black ostrich herl.
Body	Orange floss.
Rib	Broad silver tinsel edged with fine gold thread.
Hackle	A darkish cuckoo dun hackle all the way up, with a dark claret hackle near the head.
Shoulder	Kingfisher.

Wings Bright yellow macaw, with red macaw points.
Head Black ostrich herl.
Hooks 3 or 4

The Crane
Tag Silver thread and orange floss.
Tail A very long slice of bright yellow swan.
Butt Red crewel.
Body Bright medium blue floss.
Rib Silver tinsel.
Hackle A blue heron hackle all the way up.
Shoulder Gallina.
Wings Two long jungle-cock feathers with a cuckoo dun hackle over.
Head Red crewel.
Hook 2

The Crane

The Old Blue *Colour plate 6*
Tag Silver tinsel and natural coloured pig's wool.
Tail Fibres of golden pheasant tail, wood-duck, dirty red and blue swan.
Butt None.
Body Dark blue pig's wool.
Rib Silver tinsel.
Hackle Darkish blue all the way up.
Shoulder Blue jay.
Wings Two slices of dark brown turkey, with sprigs of dark green and yellow swan, peacock herl and bustard; two short jungle-cock feathers at shoulders.
Head Grey pig's wool.
Hook 3

The Blue and Orange
Tag Silver tinsel and purple floss.
Tail Sprigs of red, blue, green, and orange swan.
Butt Ruby crewel.
Body Lower two-fifths yellow orange silk floss, upper three-fifths, dark blue pig's wool.
Rib Gold thread all the way up, and in addition silver tinsel over the blue pig's wool.
Hackle Orange over the yellow and darkish blue over the blue.
Shoulder Orange-red hackle.
Wings Slices of pale blue and dirty brown swan with fibres of green, yellow, and red swan, with small slices of golden pheasant tail and speckled turkey.
Head Black ostrich herl.
Hook 3

THE NORE

The patterns for the Nore are also from Mr Staples. The Nore is more of a summer river than the Suir and the following patterns will kill well late in the season.

No. 1

Tag	Silver tinsel and olive-yellow pig's wool.
Tail	Bustard, red parrot and a topping.
Butt	None.
Body	Very dark purple-blue pig's wool (rather rough).
Rib	Silver tinsel.
Hackle	None.
Shoulder	A blue jay hackle, moderate and not too much of it.
Wings	A bunch of green peacock herl, with brown mallard over, interspersed with a little grey mallard stained light yellow or buff, and one topping over all.
Head	Olive-yellow pig's wool.
Hooks	7–12

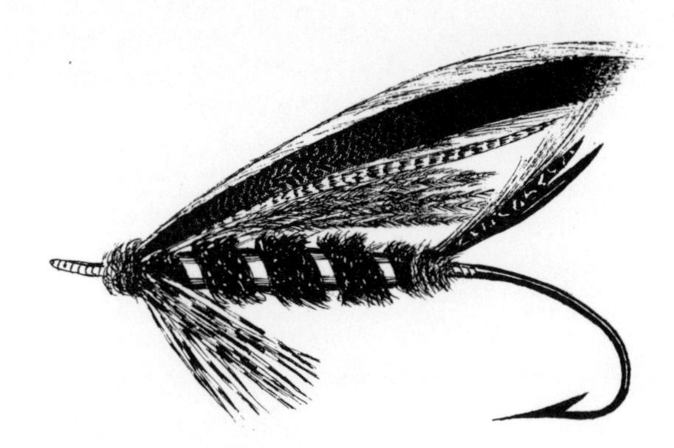

Mr Staples' No. 1

No. 2

Tag	Gold tinsel and medium blue pig's wool.
Tail	Blue macaw.
Body	(no butt) Olive-yellow pig's wool, rough and picked out at the breast.
Rib	Gold tinsel.
Hackle	None.
Shoulder	A golden olive (or rather orange) hackle with a vivid black centre.
Wings	A bunch of copper-coloured peacock herl and a good slip or two of blue macaw over it.
Head	Black.
Hooks	7–12

No. 3

Tag	Gold tinsel and light blue pig's wool.
Tail	Blue jay and fibres of a buff hackle.
Body	(no butt) Dark red (tending to claret) pig's wool, rough and picked out.
Rib	Gold tinsel.
Hackle	None.
Shoulder	A lightish blue hackle.
Wings	A bunch of copper-coloured peacock herls with slips of blue and red macaw over it.
Head	Black.
Hooks	7–12

No. 4

This is a small Galway pattern.

Tag	Gold twist and orange floss.
Tail	A topping.
Body	(no butt) Lake floss.
Rib	Fine silver tinsel.
Hackle	Gallina, trimmed on the breast.
Shoulder	A turn or two of blue jay.
Wings	A mixed wing of golden pheasant tail, gallina, tippet, bustard, mallard, and green swan sprigs.
Horns	Blue macaw with a short kingfisher feather over at the head.
Head	Black.
Hooks	7–12

THE BUSH

The Bush is a small and not very interesting river, being dull and heavy and wanting in that briskness of stream and broken water which the experienced salmon fisher loves to see; but like many other rivers of the same nature, it often holds a large quantity of fish, and in suitable weather gives very good takes to the rod. It was a favourite river with Dr Peard who rented it, and who speaks very warmly of it in *The Year of Liberty*.

The following four flies were made for me through the agency of my friend Mr Brady, by Wm Doherty and Son, fly-tyers, of Bushmills.

The Butcher Fly

This is not the fly known elsewhere as 'The Butcher'.

Tag	Silver thread and light orange floss.
Tail	Two or three tippet fibres, blue macaw and mallard.
Butt	Black ostrich herl.
Body	Dark red claret mohair.
Rib	Narrow silver tinsel.
Hackle	Dark red claret, the same shade as the body.
Shoulder	A light blue hackle.
Wings	Brown mallard.
Horns	Blue macaw.
Head	Black.
Hooks	6 or 7

The Judge

Tag	Silver thread and light orange floss.
Tail	A topping.
Butt	Peacock herl.
Body	Silver tinsel.
Rib	None.
Hackle	Golden-olive or yellow-orange (the colour is something between these two).
Shoulder	Red orange with blue jay over it.
Wings	Mixed wings of peacock and bustard, with a few fibres of tippet, and two toppings over.
Horns	Blue macaw.
Head	Peacock herl.
Hooks	6 or 7

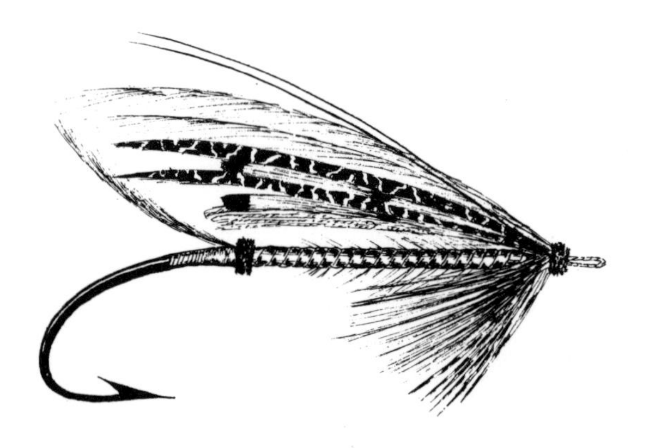

The Judge

The McGildowny

Tag	Silver thread and light orange floss.
Tail	Two or three fibres of tippet, blue macaw and mallard.
Butt	Peacock herl.
Body	Two turns of light orange floss, the rest yellow mohair.
Rib	Narrow silver tinsel.
Hackle	A dirty medium brickdust red, dressed from two-thirds down.
Shoulder	Blue jay.
Wings	Mixed bustard, mallard, tippet (plentiful), and a little peacock.
Head	Peacock herl.
Hooks	6 or 7

The Erly

This is the same as the Butcher Fly, save that the butt is yellow mohair; the body and hackle are some two shades lighter, and there is a tippet feather for an under wing. Hooks 6 or 7.

The following two flies are from Farlow's:

Powell's Fancy

Tag	Gold tinsel and orange floss.
Tail	A topping.
Butt	Peacock herl.
Body	Two turns of orange floss, the rest orange pig's wool (lighter towards the tail, darker towards the shoulder).
Rib	Gold tinsel with narrow red thread just above and beside it.
Hackle	Bright red orange.
Shoulder	Blue jay.

Wings	Golden pheasant tail, florican bustard, brown mallard, some tippet, grey mallard stained yellow, and wood-duck.
Horns	Red macaw.
Head	Black.
Hooks	6–8

The Grace

Tag	Gold tinsel and yellow floss.
Tail	A topping.
Butt	Black ostrich herl.
Body	Dark rich ruby floss.
Rib	Thick gold twist.
Hackle	Bright reddish claret.
Shoulder	A medium orange hackle with blue jay over it.
Wings	Peacock, golden pheasant tail, bustard and wood-duck, and a topping over all.
Horns	Blue macaw.
Head	Black.
Hooks	6–8

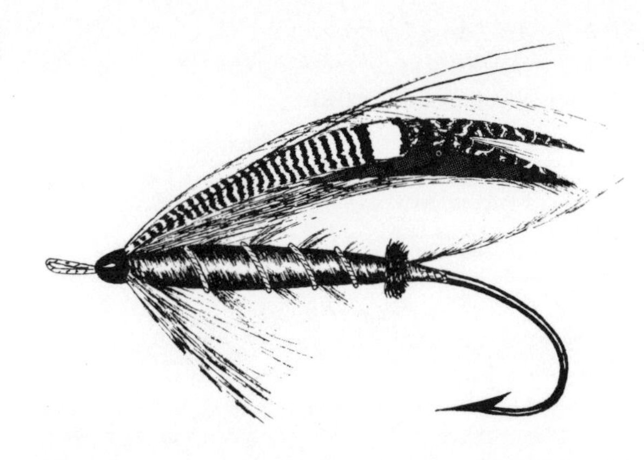

The Grace

THE BANN

The following four flies are also by William Doherty and Son:

The Garibaldi Fly

This invention of Doherty's is a showy-looking fly tied in three joints.

Tag	Silver thread and lemon floss.
Tail	A topping.
Butt	Green peacock herl.
Body	Three joints, the first yellow-orange floss, the second a shade redder orange, the third joint is the same as the second.
Rib	Three turns of silver thread at the joints.
Hackle	At the first joint (above the silver thread) a yellowish-olive hackle with a green peacock herl above it; at the second joint a shade redder orange hackle with green peacock herl above it (as before). Over the third joint a light claret hackle.
Shoulder	Blue jay.
Wings	Under wing, two good-size tippet feathers; slips of brown turkey on either side, and a topping over all.
Horns	Blue and red macaw.
Head	Green peacock herl.
Hooks	4–7

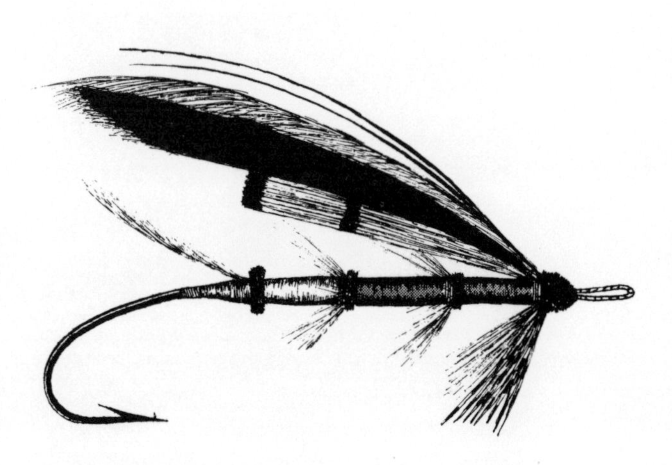

The Garibaldi Fly

The Golden Olive Fly

This is a Ballyshannon pattern; at least a fly much resembling it is used there.

Tag	Silver thread and medium blue floss.
Tail	A topping.
Butt	Black ostrich herl.
Body	Golden-yellow floss.
Rib	Gold tinsel and gold thread side by side.
Hackle	Golden olive.
Shoulder	Blue jay.
Wings	Mixed wings of bustard, grey mallard, and peacock, a few fibres of tippet and red parrot, and a topping over all.
Horns	Red and blue macaw ribs.
Head	Black.
Hooks	4–7

The Green Grouse

Tag	Gold thread and reddish orange floss.
Tail	A topping.
Butt	Brown ostrich herl.
Body	Pea-green floss.
Rib	Narrow gold tinsel.
Hackle	Grouse.
Shoulder	A yellow-olive hackle.
Wings	Mixed wings of bustard, grey mallard and tippet, and a topping over all.
Horns	Blue macaw.
Head	Black ostrich herl.
Hooks	4–7

The Blue Jay

This is the Blue Doctor dressed with Blue jay instead of blue hackle, with a mixed wing as in the Golden Olive Fly, and one topping.

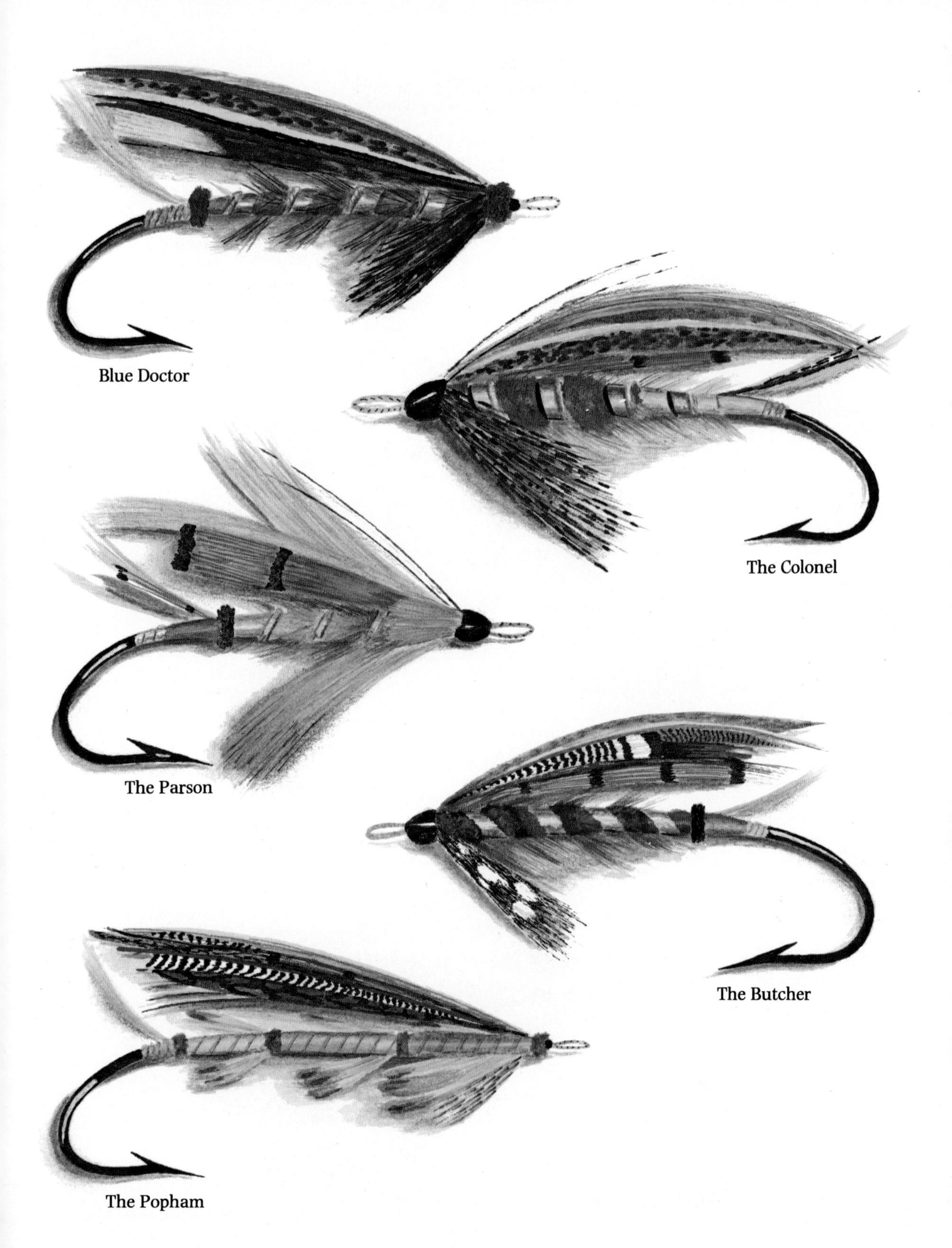

PLATE 1

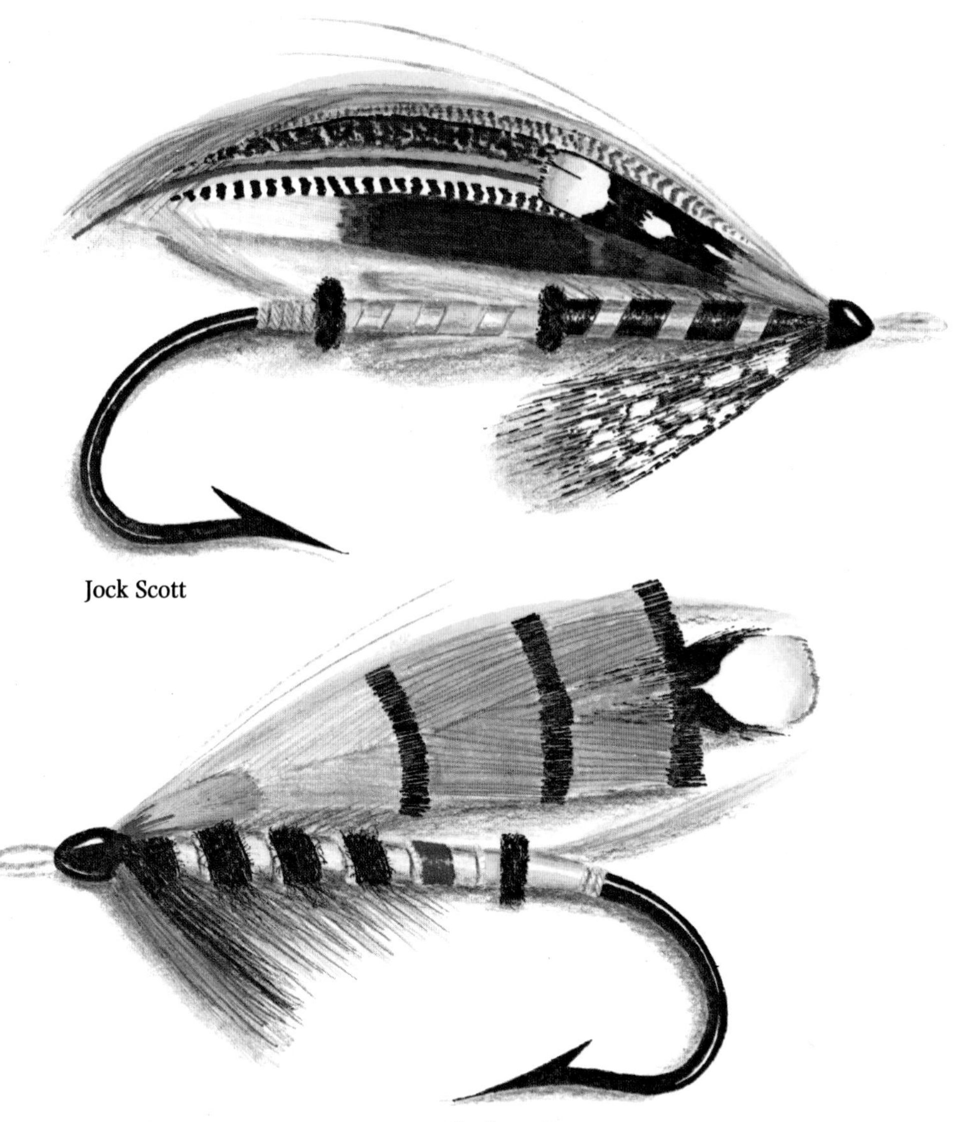

Jock Scott

Durham Ranger

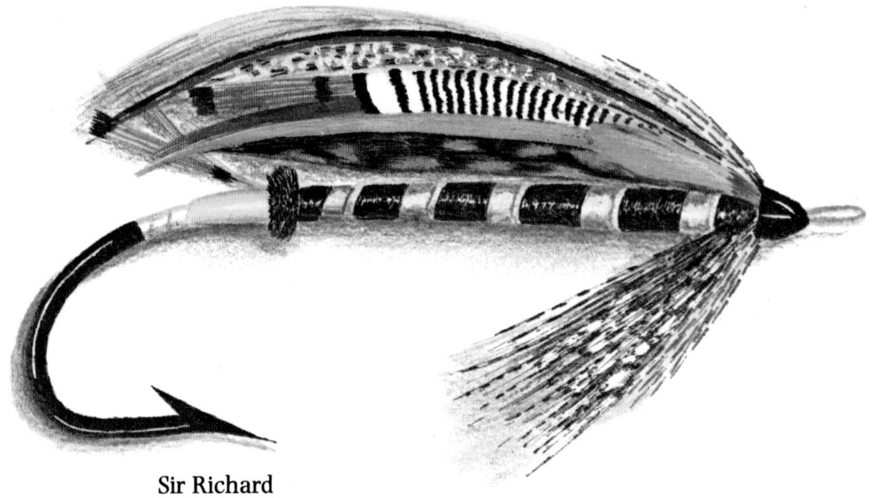

Sir Richard

PLATE 2

The Tartan

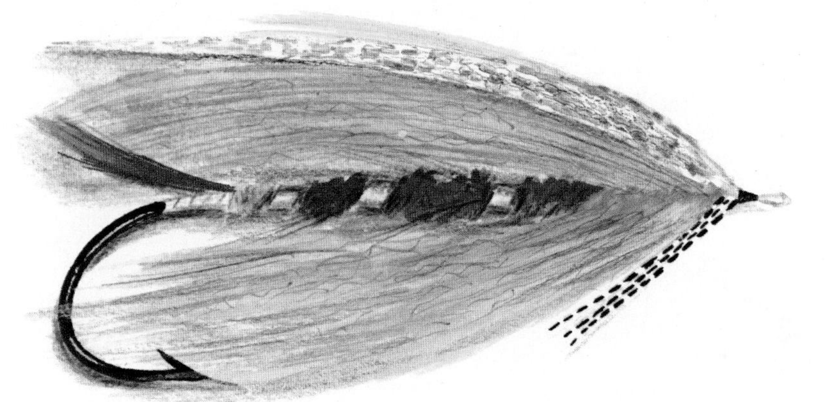

The Eagle

The Gled Wing

PLATE 3
DEE STRIP-WING FLIES

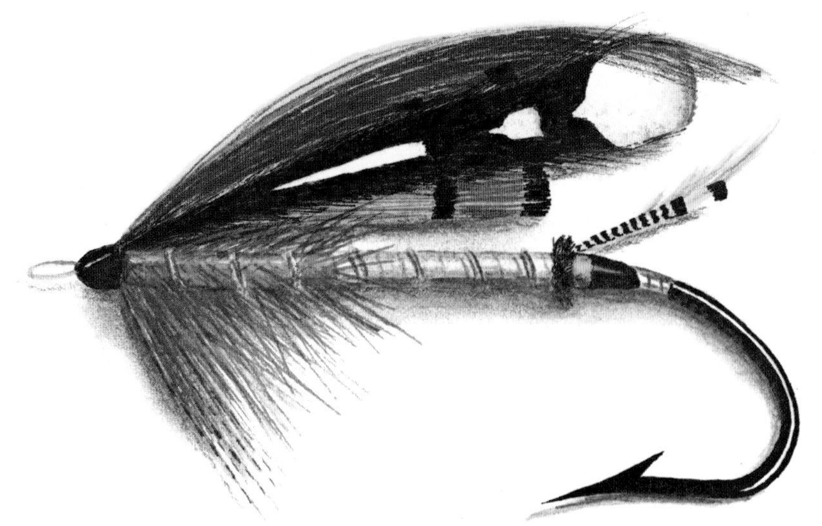
The Denison

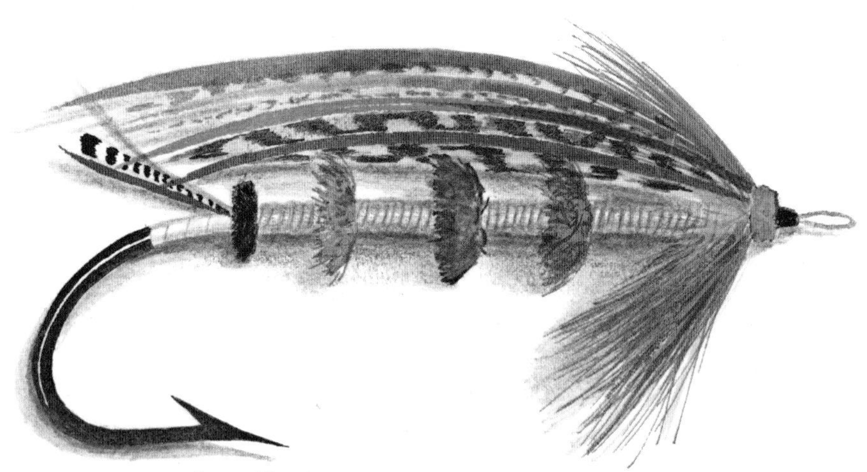
Snow Fly

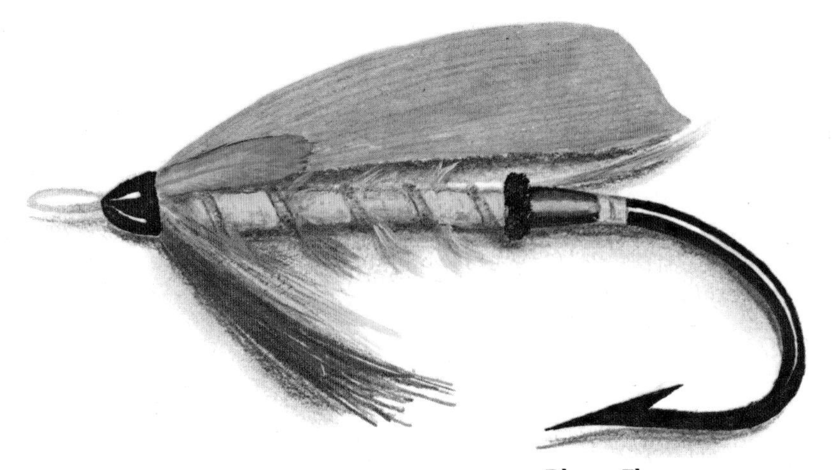
Dhoon Fly

PLATE 4

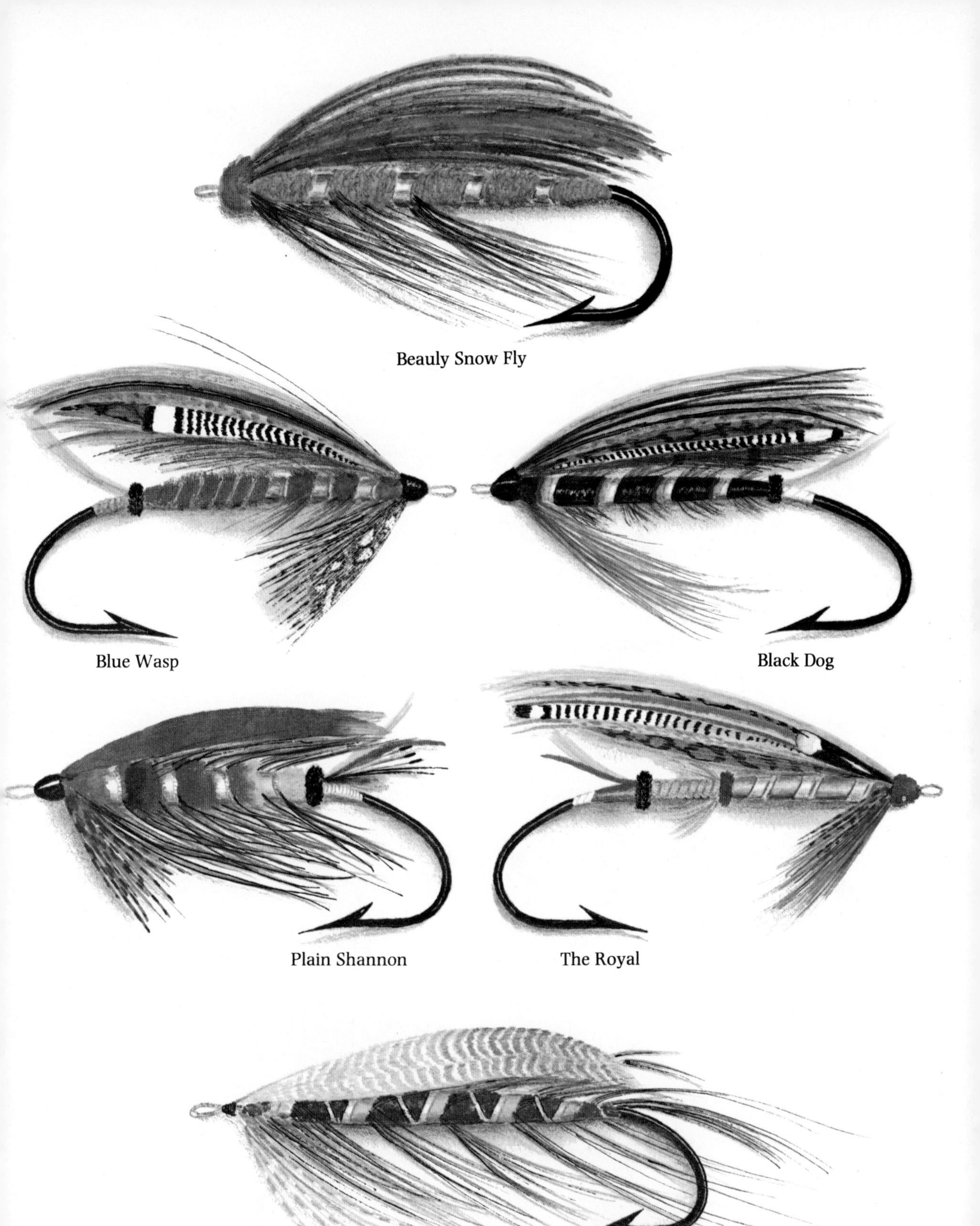
Beauly Snow Fly
Blue Wasp
Black Dog
Plain Shannon
The Royal
Purple King

PLATE 5

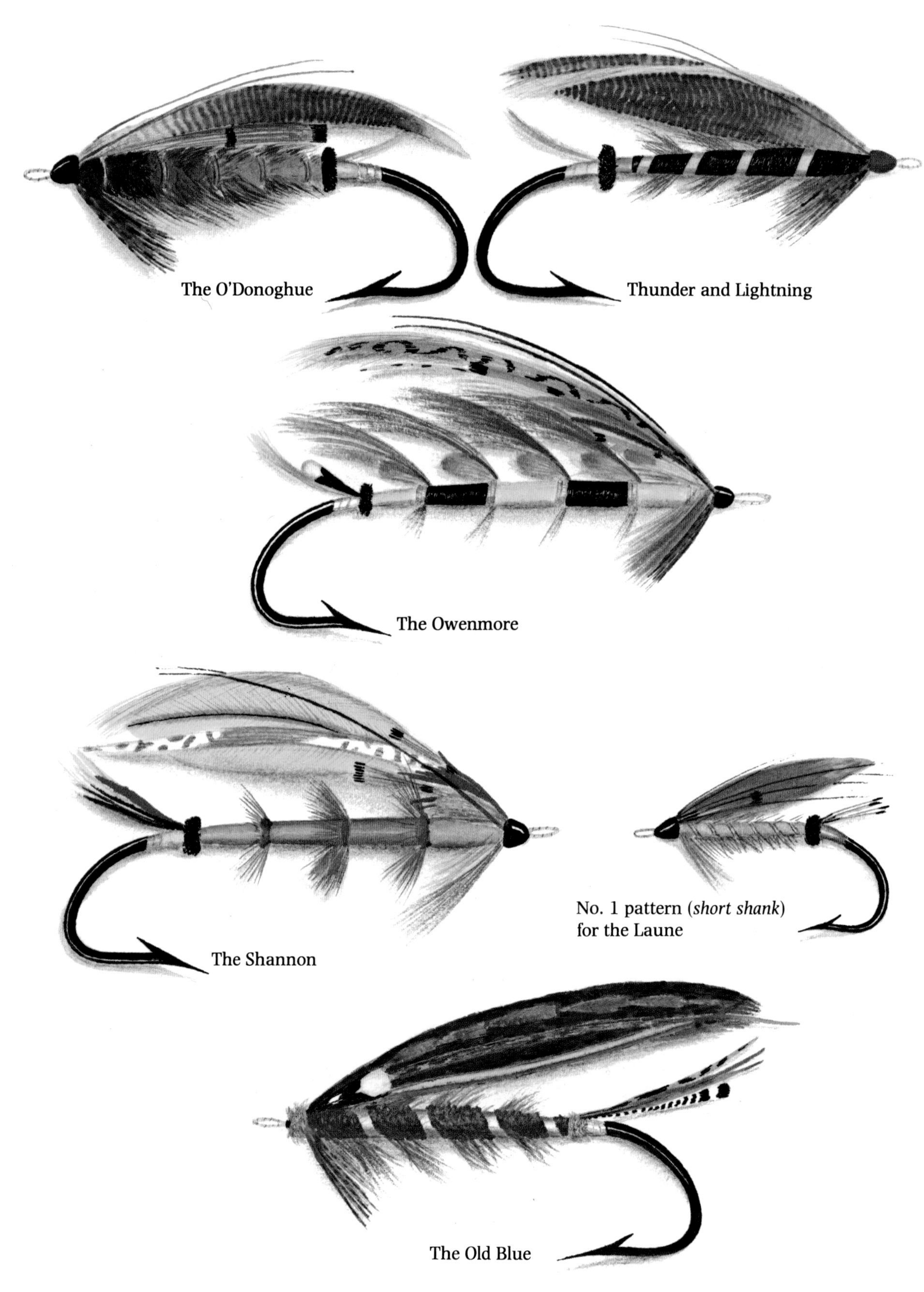
The O'Donoghue
Thunder and Lightning
The Owenmore
The Shannon
No. 1 pattern (*short shank*)
for the Laune
The Old Blue

PLATE 6

The Bittern
Francis' Favourite
Welshman's Fairy
The Blackwall
Golden River Fly
Black Joke
Morgan's Fly
No. 2 pattern for the Dee (Welsh)

PLATE 7

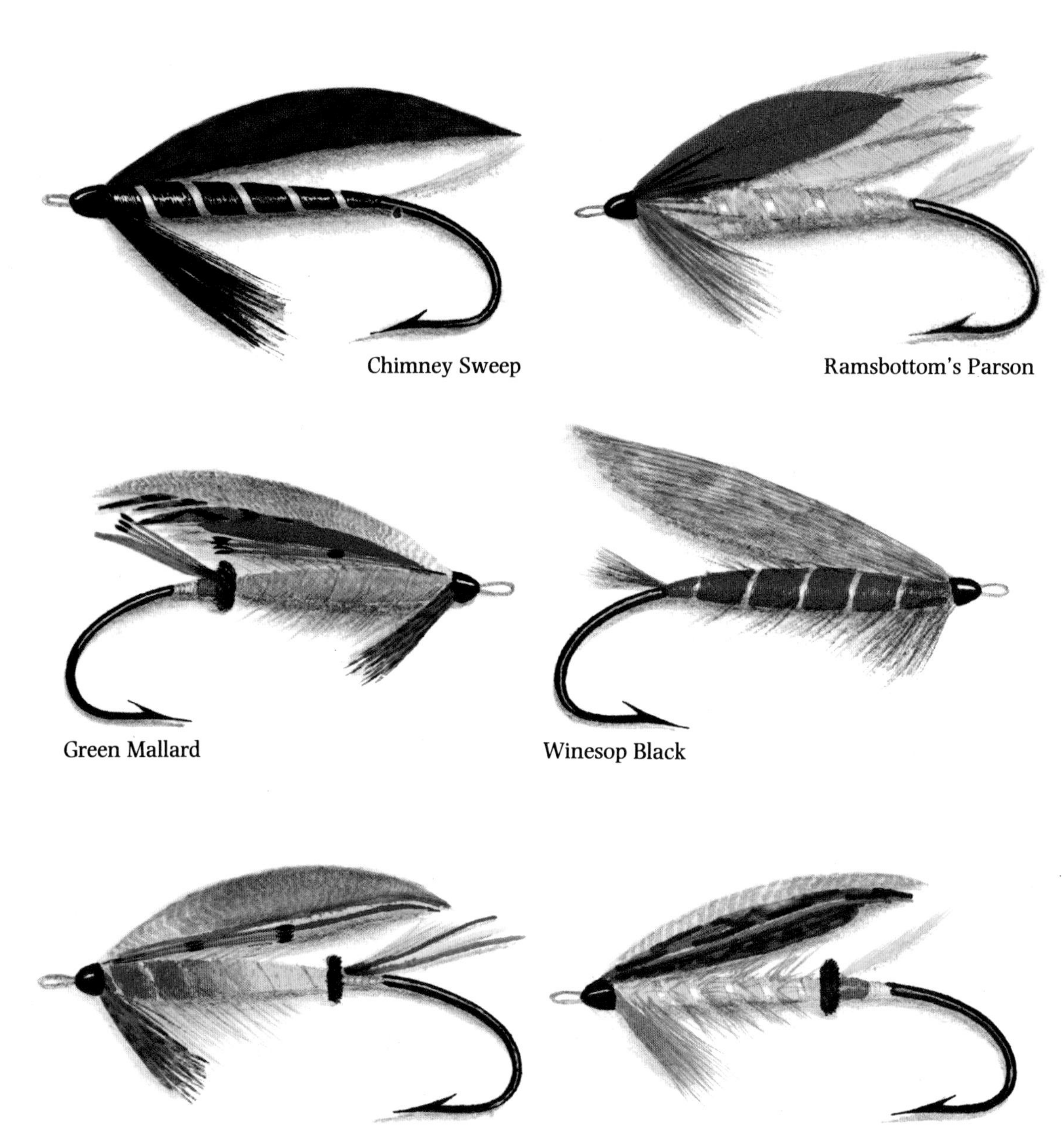
Chimney Sweep
Ramsbottom's Parson
Green Mallard
Winesop Black
No. 2 pattern for the Tyne
No. 2 pattern for the Taw & Torridge

PLATE 8

Chapter Four

Flies for Welsh and English Rivers

THE USK

Thanks to Mr Berrington, the energetic and able chairman of the Usk Board of Conservators, whose assistance to me has been most valuable, and to Mr Alfred Crawshay who is very well known as an experienced salmon angler on the Usk banks, I am uncommonly well stocked up with the latest patterns for this capital river. The Usk is one of the best managed rivers, and perhaps more salmon yearly fall to the rod there than in nearly all the other rivers south of the Scottish border put together. In the season of 1879 over 3000 salmon were killed with the rod, and in spite of a perfect generation of poachers all over the river, and benches of magistrates whose feelings in too many instances have been against the salmon laws, the Usk keeps its foremost place by hard work and good management.

The Usk flies are not gaudy as a rule; plain yellow-orange, and olive wool bodies with turkey or peacock herl wings and lightly tinselled, do best. Mr Berrington sent me two dozen flies, and Mr A. Crawshay a lot more, only a few of which I could possibly find room for. The first lot are for high water; the sizes run from 4 down to 9 accordingly as required. The bodies of all this batch are of a tawny yellow, a sort of lion-coloured wool, rather rough, some heavily ribbed, some lightly ribbed, and some without any. The tails are mostly a twitch of scarlet mohair with a bit of tippet or jungle cock. The hackles are of a dirty-brown red hard upon cinnamon, one or two with a turn of black at the shoulder. The wings are either plain brown speckled turkey, bustard, or bunches of peacock herl.

The next batch run 6, 7, and 8. The bodies are of warm orange wool; tails as before; pretty closely ribbed; with cock-y-bonddu hackles. The wings are either of dark rich brown turkey or a bunch of herl. Berrington's Favourite is dressed in this way; the hackle is a coch-y-bonddu with a black centre, and a rich brown turkey wing, with a slip of the light tip turkey (as used in the Toppy wing) between.

Some flies are called *grubs*. They are dressed without wings, merely as hackles. They have these hackles, one at the head, one in the middle, and a third near the tail; sometimes these will be all dusty red, or a coch-y-bonddu at the head, a red in the middle, and a dark olive at the tail. They have no rib and the bodies are tawny-orange or olive. Hooks, 6, 7, and 8.

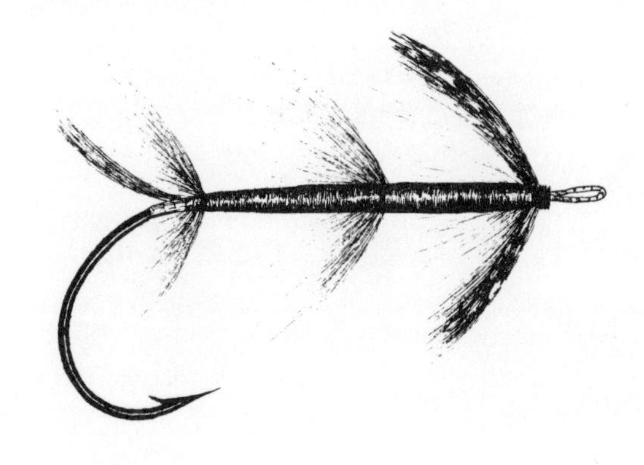

A typical grub fly

I killed a good many fish a few years since on the Usk, and all with one fly which was thence called:

Francis's Favourite *Colour plate 7*

Tail	Tippet and a bit of ibis. (No tag or butt.)
Body	A few turns of yellow wool and the rest of dark claret wool.
Rib	Gold thread.
Hackle	A longish coch-y-bonddu hackle, black at the butt, ending on the shoulder.
Shoulder	See hackle.
Wings	Dark speckled turkey.
Head	Black.
Hooks	6–8

The Hornets

These have fat bodies dressed after the fashion of the 'bumble' trout fly; peacock herl and yellow or orange crewel, alternately; coch-y-bonddu hackle at the shoulder, and brown turkey wings. Hooks, 7 or 8.

Low water patterns have medium olive wool bodies and hackles of the same shade; silver tinsel rib; tail, scarlet mohair or with jungle-cock. The wings are a bunch of herl or a bit of darkish bustard. Hooks, 6 or 7. All these flies have peacock herl heads, and are for the lower division of the river. Higher up, Mr Crawshay's patterns come in. He has adopted the Tweed plan of using double hooks and it has answered well.

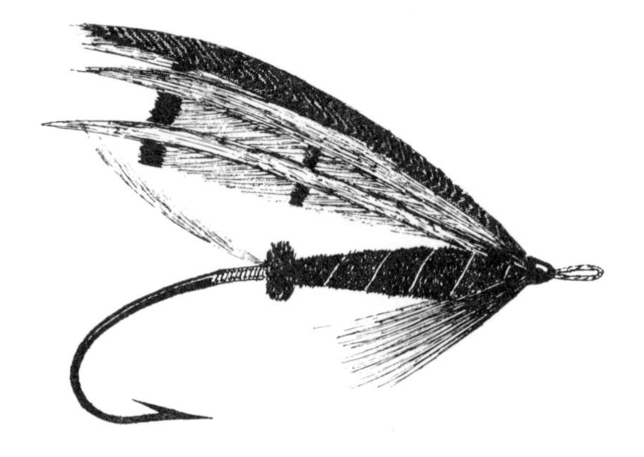

Mr Crawshay's No. 1

Here are his patterns:

No. 1

Tag	Silver twist.
Tail	A topping.
Butt	Black ostrich.
Body	Black wool.
Rib	Silver thread.
Hackle	None.
Shoulder	A magenta hackle.
Wings	Two large tippet feathers, some strips of light turkey dyed yellow, with brown mallard over.
Head	Black.
Hooks	6–8, single or double.

No. 2

Tag	Silver twist.
Tail	A topping.
Butt	Black ostrich herl.
Body	Two turns of orange floss, the rest black wool.
Rib	None.
Hackle	Black all the way up.
Shoulder	Darkish blue.
Wings	Tippet sprigs, some blue and red macaw, a little golden pheasant tail, and some brown mallard.
Head	Black.
Hooks	6–8, single or double.

No. 3

Tag	Silver twist.
Tail	A topping.
Butt	Black ostrich herl.
Body	Dark olive wool.
Rib	Gold tinsel (moderate).
Hackle	A natural dark-brownish red hackle.
Shoulder	Blue jay.
Wings	Mixed wings of tippet, wood-duck, brown mallard, and buff and lavender swan.
Head	Black.
Hooks	6–8, single or double.

THE WYE

In recent years the Wye has become a very different river. The netting has been so close that the angling has been all but destroyed, and the upper waters are nearly abandoned by the disgusted proprietary to the poachers who have a great time of it in the spawning season.*
The accompanying patterns come from Captain Hotchkiss, a great authority on the river, and were procured for me by Mr Berrington. The first is the Bittern, followed by others without names.

The Bittern *Colour plate 7*

Tag	Silver tinsel.
Tail	A topping, wood-duck and ibis.
Body	(no butt) Bright golden floss, rather full.
Rib	None.
Hackle	A longish and full hackle of a peculiar shade of olive-yellow which is obtained by staining a medium blue dun a pale yellow, this gives it an olive greenish-yellow tint of a very taking look.
Wings	Two good clearly marked bittern hackles and one topping over. (The best bittern hackles to use are those of a yellowish tint and on which the ribbed markings are most distinct.)
Head	Black.
Hooks	6–8

Now for the un-named breed:

No. 1
This is dressed after the fashion of the Bittern, the body, however, being of the same colour as the flesh of a cooked salmon; the hackle is a long and full blue dun, and the wing and tail is the same as in The Bittern.

No. 2
This one is said to be a first-rate killer throughout the season.

Tag	Silver twist.
Tail	A topping and a bit of ibis.
Body	(no butt) Bright canary yellow wool.
Rib	Doubled gold thread.
Hackle	Hackled very thickly with two bright orange hackles laid together, ending on the shoulder.
Shoulder	See hackle.
Wings	Two tippet feathers, with bustard and golden pheasant tail over.
Horns	Blue macaw.
Head	Black.
Hook	8

*The Wye has made a remarkable recovery since this was written.

No. 3

Tag	Silver twist and pale blue floss.
Tail	A topping.
Butt	Black ostrich herl.
Body	A dark yellow, nearer to orange.
Rib	Broad gold tinsel.
Hackle	A redder orange than the body.
Shoulder	A grouse hackle wound on thick.
Wings	Two tippet feathers with brown mallard over.
Horns	Red macaw.
Head	Black.
Hook	6

A good spring fly.

No. 4
Another spring fly.

Tag	Silver twist.
Tail	A little wood-duck and ibis.
Butt	None.
Body	Rough light blue wool.
Rib	Fine silver tinsel.
Hackle	A natural smoky-blue dun hackle, ending on the shoulder.
Shoulder	See hackle.
Wings	Speckled light brown turkey, with long sprigs of wood-duck over.
Head	Black.
Hook	7

No. 5
This one is an autumn fly.

Tag	Silver twist.
Tail	A small topping, a bit of tippet, and a sprig of teal.
Butt	None.

Body One turn of yellow wool, the rest of rough reddish claret wool, with a little bit of lightish blue at the shoulder.
Rib Fine silver tinsel.
Hackle None.
Shoulder A black hackle.
Wings Sprigs of light yellow and red swan, slips of bustard, florican bustard, and turkey mixed; brown mallard veiled over.
Cheeks Short jungle-cock.
Horns Blue macaw.
Head Black.
Hook 6

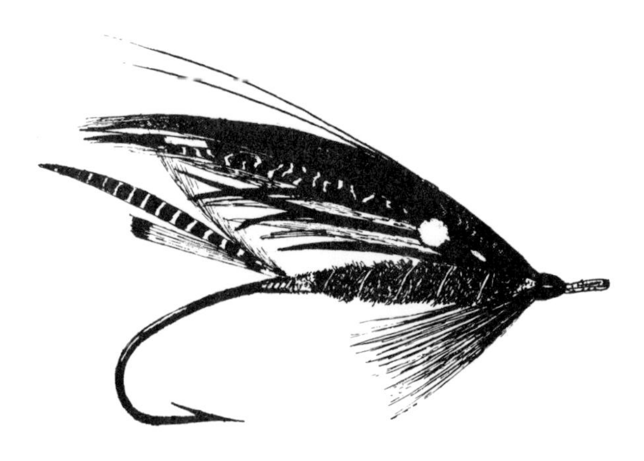

Captain Hotchkiss' No. 5

No. 6
Tag Gold tinsel.
Tail A topping and ibis.
Butt None.
Body Burnt sienna brown wool, dressed fattish.
Rib Gold thread.
Hackle A coch-y-bonddu hackle all the way up, ending on the shoulder.
Shoulder See hackle.
Wings Two tippet feathers for the under wing, then slices of golden pheasant tail, and brown mallard over.
Head Black.
Hook 8

All Captain Hotchkiss' flies can be dressed on double hooks of the sneck bend pattern.

THE DOVEY OR DYFI

The Welshman's Fairy *Colour plate 7*
Tag Gold tinsel and orange floss.
Tail A topping and some gallina stained pink.
Butt Black ostrich herl.
Body Red wool.
Rib Silver tinsel.
Hackle Two hackles: claret and golden olive laid on together and wound on simultaneously. This will be found easiest to do either by stripping one side of the hackle, or preparing the hackles and laying one within the other.
Shoulder An unstained pale-blue dun hackle.
Wings Strips of mallard, brown mottled turkey, florican bustard, gallina, and pale dirty pink swan.
Horns Blue macaw.
Head Black.
Hooks 6–10

The Dovey Captain
This is a jointed fly.
Tag Gold thread.
Tail A topping and tippet.
Butt Black ostrich herl.
Body In four joints, all of floss silk. The first joint is composed of one half dark orange and the other half of dark red. The next joint is bright yellow and dark red. The third and fourth joints are of yellow and black floss.
Rib A few turns of fine gold thread below each joint.
Hackle A small cock of the rock feather would on as a hackle above each of the turns of gold thread.
Shoulder Blue jay.
Wings Brown mottled turkey with brown mallard over.
Horns Blue macaw.
Head Black.
Hooks 6–10, or even smaller in low water.

The above two patterns were from Farlow's.

THE CONWAY

The following patterns were sent to me by C. Blackwall, Esq., the secretary of the Conway Club; and the patterns may therefore be thoroughly relied on. They are all capital general flies that would kill on many rivers.

The Blackwall *Colour plate 7*

Tag	Silver thread and medium blue floss.
Tail	A topping and a small blue chatterer (or kingfisher) feather.
Butt	Black ostrich herl.
Body	Half medium orange floss, half redder orange mohair.
Rib	Broad silver tinsel.
Hackle	Claret.
Shoulder	A short wood-duck hackle.
Wings	Two medium jungle-cock, tippet sprigs, slips of wood-duck and two toppings.
Horns	Blue macaw.
Head	Black.
Hooks	5–9

This is Mr Blackwall's own fancy, said to be very deadly, and I have given his name to it; alas, the rest have no names.

No. 1

Tag	Silver thread and medium blue floss.
Tail	Sprigs of yellow swan, wood-duck, and blue jay.
Butt	Black ostrich herl.
Body	One-third yellow floss, the rest olive-green with a few strands of yellow pig's wool.
Rib	Silver tinsel.
Hackle	Lightish claret.
Shoulder	Blue jay.
Wings	Two medium-length jungle-cock feathers, sprigs of tippet, wood-duck (plenty), a strip of red swan, and plenty of golden pheasant tail.
Horns	Blue macaw.
Head	Black.
Hooks	5–9

No. 2

Tag	Silver thread and medium blue floss.
Tail	A topping with slips of wood-duck.
Butt	Black ostrich herl.
Body	Medium orange floss.
Rib	Silver tinsel.
Hackle	Coch-y-bonddu stained claret.
Shoulder	Blue jay.
Wings	Tippet fibres, slips of wood-duck, and golden pheasant tail over.
Horns	Blue and red macaw.
Head	Black.
Hooks	5–9

This is the old Conway pattern.

No. 3

Tag	Silver thread and yellow floss.
Tail	Yellow swan, tippet and wood-duck sprigs.
Butt	Black ostrich herl.
Body	Lightish medium blue floss.
Rib	Silver tinsel.
Hackle	Lightish medium blue (the same shade as the body), and a little short wood-duck at the breast as a hackle.
Shoulder	A tippet feather tied in as a hackle over the wood-duck.
Wings	Two medium jungle-cock feathers, slips of tippet, golden pheasant tail over this, and short wood-duck slips over that.
Head	Black.
Hooks	5–9

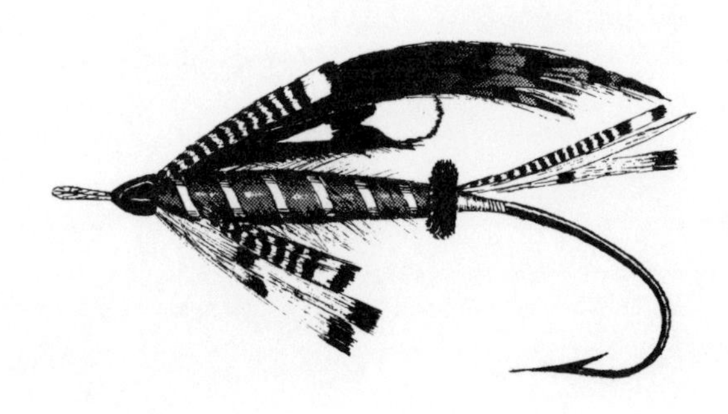

Mr Blackwall's No. 3

No. 4

Tag	Silver thread and medium blue floss.
Tail	A topping and some wood-duck.
Butt	Black ostrich herl.
Body	Silver tinsel.
Rib	See hackle.
Hackle	A dark claret hackle with a strand of yellow silk laid on under and beside it.
Shoulder	Blue jay.
Wings	Plenty of wood-duck slips with tippet sprigs over; over this, brown mallard and golden pheasant tail, and a sprig or two of yellow-olive swan.
Horns	Blue macaw.
Head	Black.
Hooks	5–9

THE COTHI

The following two flies for the Cothi were forwarded by Mr Harrison of Lampeter, and the patterns are good both for salmon and sewin.

Mr Benyon's pattern

No. 1

Tag	Silver tinsel.
Tail	Scarlet ibis.
Body	Blotting-paper red crewel.
Rib	Narrow silver tinsel.
Hackle	Pale lemon ending on the shoulder.
Wings	Light speckled turkey stained a bright ochre-yellow.
Head	Black.
Hooks	9–11

No. 2

Tag	Silver tinsel.
Tail	Scarlet ibis.
Body	Light yellow crewel.
Rib	Narrow silver tinsel.
Hackle	Pale lemon ending on the shoulder.
Wings	Two slips of blue macaw and two of white-tipped black turkey.
Head	Black.
Hooks	9–11

Here is one still more inharmonious. It comes from Mr Benyon, who says that it was sent to him by an experienced hand on the river.

Tag	Gold tinsel.
Tail	Some yellow-green parrot and a bit of drake dyed yellow.
Body	A sort of magenta-claret floss.
Rib	Fine gold tinsel.
Hackle	Pale lemon ending on the shoulder.
Wings	Bright sky-blue swan.
Head	Black.
Hooks	9–11

It certainly is a curio.

THE TAFF

These patterns are also from Mr Benyon, an *habitué* of the river.*

The Trewern Tickler
This old standard favourite has no tail to it.

Body Darkish medium blue wool.
Rib Silver tinsel.
Hackle A black hackle starting two-thirds down.
Shoulder Blue jay.
Wings A tippet feather with brown mallard veiled over.
Head Black ostrich herl.
Hooks 7–9 single or double.

Now for the rest which have no names and are dressed without butts.

No. 1

Tag Silver tinsel and orange floss.
Tail A topping.
Body Half medium blue wool and half dark burnt sienna brown wool.
Rib Silver tinsel.
Hackle None.
Shoulder Gallina hackle.
Wings Mixed fibres of tippet, speckled peacock, golden pheasant tail and rump feather, bustard, yellow swan, and three or four strands of emerald peacock herl.
Head Black ostrich herl.
Hooks 7–9

No. 2
This is Mr Benyon's pet.

Tag Silver tinsel.
Tail Lemon yellow swan.
Body A lightish dirty yellow wool.
Rib Broad gold tinsel.
Hackle Black starting half-way down.
Shoulder A brown bustard hackle.
Wings A short tippet, shreds of bustard, golden pheasant tail, gallina, and one or two fibres of yellow and orange swan.

*Alas, the Taff is no longer a salmon river.

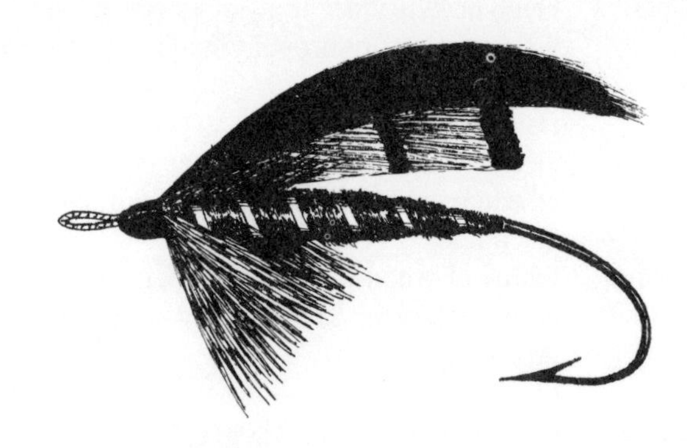

The Trewern Tickler

Horns Blue macaw.
Head Black ostrich herl.
Hooks 6 or 7

No. 3
This is a curious beast.

Tag Fine gold twist.
Tail A topping.
Body One-third yellow-orange floss, the rest of pale blue floss.
Rib Silver tinsel.
Hackle A yellow-orange hackle over the lower joint, and a jay hackle over the blue joint.
Shoulder A claret hackle.
Wings Some tippet and sprigs of golden pheasant rump feather, golden pheasant tail, and brown mallard with a little wood-duck and blue and red macaw.
Head Black ostrich herl.
Hooks Double hooks 7–9

No. 4
This is the best autumn fly. It is, in fact, the old Fiery Brown.

Tag Silver twist.
Tail Red ibis.

Body Fiery brown wool that looks red when you look at it but brown when held up to the light.
Rib Gold tinsel.
Hackle Fiery brown the same shade as the body, all the way up ending on the shoulder.
Shoulder See hackle.
Wings Fibres of wood-duck and tippet, brown mallard, blue and red macaw, and some green parrot.
Head Black.
Hooks Double hooks 7–9

THE TIVEY OR TEIFI, AND TOWY

These are all the latest patterns and were procured for me by Mr Berrington, from Mr Brigstocke, formerly the secretary to the Tivey Board. They are the handiwork of Colonel Lewes of Landyssul who is the chairman of the Tivey Board, and one of the keenest and best rods on the river.

The Black Joke *Colour plate 7*

Tag Gold twist.
Tail A topping
Butt Black ostrich herl.
Body Black floss.
Rib Doubled fine gold twist with fine scarlet silk between.
Hackle None.
Shoulder Blue jay.
Wings Brown speckled turkey dipped in onion dye, and common cock-pheasant tail.
Horns Red macaw.
Head Black.
Hooks 6 or 7

The Saville

Tag Silver tinsel.
Tail A topping and a short Indian crow feather.
Butt None.
Body Half orange-claret and half medium blue, floss or wool.
Rib Gold thread.
Hackle Claret starting two-thirds down.
Shoulder Blue jay.
Wings Mixed sprigs of tippet, golden pheasant rump feather, dark bustard, some bittern wing, and a little pintail or teal over; over that, golden pheasant tail and brown mallard, and a topping over all.
Cheeks Short jungle-cock.
Horns Blue macaw.
Head Black.
Hooks 6 or 7

Cock of Heullan Falls

Tag Fine gold twist.
Tail A topping.
Butt Scarlet crewel.
Body Half dark orange wool, and half claret wool.
Rib Medium gold tinsel.
Hackle Claret over the claret wool.
Shoulder Gallina dipped in onion dye.
Wings Mixed fibres of tippet, golden pheasant tail, black partridge, yellow, and lake swan, with golden pheasant tail and bittern wing over, then slips of brown mallard over that.
Horns Blue macaw.
Head Black.
Hooks 6 or 7

The Captain (Tivey)

Tag Gold tinsel.
Tail A topping and a few peacock sword feather herls.
Butt None.
Body Dark orange crewel.
Rib Fine gold tinsel.
Hackle A common red cock's hackle all the way up, with some brown mallard and long sprigs of peacock sword feather tied in at the breast and shoulder.
Shoulder See hackle.

Wings Two tippet feathers with darkish bittern over.
Head Black.
Hooks 6 or 7

The Colonel (Tivey)
Tag Silver twist.
Tail Black partridge with two fibres each of ibis and yellow macaw.
Butt None.
Body Four-fifths of darkish cinnamon crewel and one-fifth at shoulder of lake-red crewel.
Rib Silver thread.
Hackle Claret all the way up.
Shoulder Blue jay.
Wings A golden pheasant rump feather and a few small bronze fibres of peacock herl, then dark brown speckled turkey and a little bustard.
Horns Blue macaw.
Head Black.
Hooks 6 or 7

The Golden River Fly *Colour plate 7*
This pattern originates from North America.
Tag Gold twist and gold floss.
Tail A topping.
Butt None.
Body Half dark blue wool and half claret wool.
Rib Gold tinsel.
Hackle Claret all the way up.
Shoulder Blue jay.
Wings Two tippet feathers with brown speckled turkey over, and a topping over all.
Head Black.
Hook 8
A very good fly on the Tivey.

Here is a very good fly from Mr J. D. Pryse of Bwlchlychan.
Tag Gold tinsel and puce floss.
Tail A topping.
Butt Black ostrich herl.
Body Bright orange pig's wool.

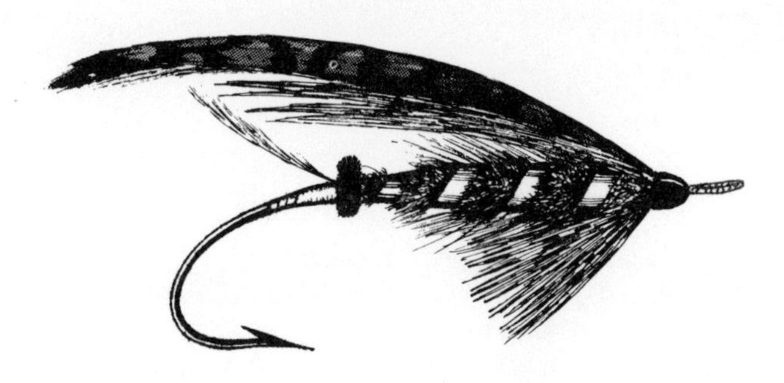

Mr Pryse's pattern

Rib Broad gold tinsel.
Hackle Bright orange same as the body.
Shoulder Blue jay.
Wings Strips of orange swan with golden pheasant tail over.
Head Black.
Hooks 6–8

Of the Towy, Mr C. Morgan of Nant-caredig, says, there are few regular standard patterns, but the Butcher, the Blue, the Silver and the Black Doctors, with Jock Scott, are the best flies that can be used. One fly which Mr Morgan states to be first-rate is the following:

Morgan's Fly *Colour plate 7*
Tag Dark claret wool.
Tail Red ibis.
Butt None.
Body A turn of the claret wool used in the tag, then the rest of light blue wool.
Rib Silver thread.
Hackle Light blue the same as the body, all the way up ending on the shoulder.
Shoulder See hackle.
Wings Brown mallard.
Head Black.
Hooks 6–8

THE DEE

The accompanying flies were sent to me by Mr Townshead of Wrexham who obtained them for me from Colonel T., a noted angler on the Dee. The Dee flies are very sober and plain and have no butts or body hackles.

No. 1

Tag	Gold tinsel.
Tail	A small tippet.
Body	Bronze peacock herl.
Rib	Gold tinsel.
Shoulder	A brown-red hackle.
Wings	A mixture of brown turkey and thin peacock herl fibres from near the 'eye' of the tail feather.
Head	Peacock herl.
Hooks	5–8

No. 2 *Colour plate 7*

This one has no tail or body hackle.

Body	Bronze peacock herl.
Rib	Gold tinsel.
Shoulder	Coch-y-bonddu.
Wings	Two short crimson-red hackles (with a lake tinge) set on either side, with a bunch of long fibres from a cock pheasant tail between them.
Head	Peacock herl.
Hooks	5–8

The old miner's No. 1

No. 3

Tag	Gold tinsel.
Tail	Sprigs of tippet.
Body	Bronze peacock herl.
Rib	Gold tinsel.
Shoulder	A dark olive brown hackle.
Wings	A bunch of fibres from the rump of a speckled brown hen with fibres of tippet on either side.
Head	Peacock herl.
Hooks	5–8

No. 4

Tag	None.
Tail	A scrap of teal stained slightly olive.
Body	Medium brown mohair.
Rib	Silver thread.
Shoulder	Coch-y-bonddu hackle.
Wings	Mottled peacock.
Horns	Mottled peacock fibres stained yellow.
Head	Peacock herl.
Hooks	5–8

THE ESK

This is a fine river, and would be even finer if the Solway stake nets were only muzzled. A good many fish go up it in summer and autumn but the fish are not taken much before the autumn, except with Stewart tackle dressed of good size, and then the fish are mostly foul hooked.

The following four flies are the best according to the cognoscenti. They were got from an old miner – who was said to be the piscatory Solomon of the river – after an expenditure of much time, patience, and whisky.

No. 1

Tag	Gold tinsel.
Tail	Some tippet and a strand or two of orange hackle.

Butt	A turn of violet crewel.
Body	A thin body of gold tinsel.
Rib	None.
Hackle	Black (not too heavy) all the way up.
Shoulder	Gallina.
Wings	First a topping and over that some wood-duck sprigs, then some of golden pheasant tail, and lastly some washed-out dun turkey, a sort of dust colour, rather more of this than the rest. The wings are not very heavy and the fibres are loose.
Head	A small head of scarlet crewel.
Hooks	4–7

No. 2

Tag	Gold tinsel.
Tail	Sprigs of tippet and wood-duck.
Butt	Dark violet crewel.
Body	Two turns of lemon coloured crewel, the rest of black crewel.
Rib	Gold thread.
Hackle	None.
Shoulder	Large spot gallina just dipped in a lemon dye.
Wings	A short point of sword feather and some tippet sprigs, over that a little grey drake, and over all two thin strips of washed-out dust coloured speckled turkey.
Head	A small head of scarlet crewel (same as No. 1).
Hook	4

No. 3

Tag	A turn of gold tinsel and two turns of deep orange floss.
Tail	Tippet sprigs and wood-duck.
Butt	Medium blue crewel.
Body	Dark reddish claret pig's wool left roughish.
Rib	Gold thread.
Hackle	None.
Shoulder	Gallina.
Wings	Two strips of dirty dun (dusty) turkey with a blotch or two in them.
Head	Black.
Hook	6

No. 4

Tag	Gold tinsel.
Tail	Tippet sprigs.
Butt	Violet crewel.
Body	Two turns of scarlet crewel, the rest of black crewel.
Rib	Gold twist.
Hackle	None.
Shoulder	A few sprigs of tippet mixed with red claret hackle fibres, with a turn of gallina over.
Wings	Spare sprigs of washed-out turkey (the colour of whitey-brown paper) with a few spare blotches on the lower half, with a few tippet sprigs under.
Head	A small head of red crewel.
Hooks	8 or 9

THE EDEN

This is one of the finest of our English rivers and if properly treated would be one of the most productive. It still produces a great quantity of salmon and affords a good deal of sport, though the minnow is often more deadly than the fly. Mr Rowell supplied me with some patterns which I have corrected to the present time by patterns which I got from Routledge, the tackle maker who was a great authority there, and who sadly departed this life when he was drowned in the River Eden in 1879.

The Chimney Sweep *Colour plate 8*

This is a very striking fly and is the only thoroughly black fly I ever saw. It is a favourite on the Eden and Mr Rowell says it will kill when none of the others will, and I shall certainly try it elsewhere. It has no tag, butt, or body hackle.

Tail	A single topping.
Body	Black floss.
Rib	Medium silver tinsel.
Shoulder	A long black hackle.
Wings	Two slips of black cockatoo tail or any black feather.
Head	Black.
Hooks	6–8

Now for some first class Eden flies which go unnamed.

No. 1

Tag	Silver tinsel.
Tail	Tippet and a little teal.
Butt	None.
Body	Bright orange floss.
Rib	Double gold twist.
Hackle	Golden olive all the way up.
Shoulder	Gallina.
Wings	Upper wing, two slips of teal and some tippet. Over wing, two slips of dark dun (cinnamon) turkey.
Head	Black.
Hooks	6–8

No. 2

Tag	Silver tinsel.
Tail	A topping.
Butt	None.
Body	Dark red floss (deep ruby), and at the shoulder a wad of wool the same colour which is picked out.
Rib	Silver tinsel and silver twist.
Hackle	A silver grey hackle with a black centre and tip, all the way up.
Shoulder	Gallina.
Wings	Tippet, teal, bustard, golden pheasant tail, and a topping over all.
Cheeks	Short jungle-cock.
Head	Black.
Hooks	6–8

No. 3 (Mr Pattison's favourite)

No. 3

This was one of the late Mr Pattison's favourite patterns. Mr Pattison was the secretary of the Angling Association.

Tag	Silver tinsel.
Tail	Some saddle feather from a golden pheasant and a fibre or two of ibis.
Butt	None.
Body	Two turns of golden floss, the rest of pale pea-green floss.
Rib	Silver tinsel.
Hackle	Black all the way up ending on shoulder.
Shoulder	See hackle.
Wings	A golden pheasant saddle feather and some tippet, with a little grey mallard and brown speckled turkey (lightish at the tip) over.
Head	Black.
Hooks	6–8

No. 4

Tag	Silver tinsel.
Tail	A bunch of yellow fibres from a parroquet (parakeet).
Butt	None.
Body	Dark blue floss with bright red wool at the shoulder.
Rib	Silver tinsel.
Hackle	Violet over two-thirds of the body, ending on the shoulder.
Shoulder	See hackle.
Wings	Some sprigs of grey mallard (drake), a bit of tippet, some golden pheasant rump, and golden pheasant saddle over, then strips of cinnamon turkey.
Head	Black.
Hooks	6–8

There is another favourite Eden fly called the Doctor Kenealy; this is a Blue Doctor with gallina at the shoulder and speckled grey turkey wings.

THE LUNE

The Lune is a latish river for angling owing to the nets and other obstructions. However, it would be one of our finest English rivers if fairly treated. The late Mr Fennell expressed a high opinion of its capabilities.

Mr Naylor of Keighley sent me the following patterns, having procured them from a gentleman who lives on the banks of the river and who regularly fishes it with much success. The flies are characteristic, being all of the same stamp, with dark turkey wings and without butts.

No. 1

Tag	Gold tinsel.
Tail	A few tippet fibres.
Body	Bright orange floss.
Rib	Narrow gold tinsel.
Hackle	Deep red orange all the way up.
Shoulder	Gallina.
Wings	Slices of brown speckled turkey, or feathers from a pea-hen's back.
Head	Black.
Hooks	6–8

No. 2

Tag	Gold tinsel.
Tail	The point of a small orange-yellow hackle and a little bit of ibis.
Body	Half darkish blue floss and half claret pig's wool.
Rib	Narrow gold tinsel.
Hackle	Claret all the way up.
Shoulder	A dusty brick red hackle.
Wings	Slices of brown speckled feather (as in No. 1).
Head	Black.
Hooks	6–8

No. 3

Tag	Gold tinsel.
Tail	A small orange-yellow hackle point and a little ibis (as in No. 2).
Body	Darkish lake floss, almost a carbuncle colour.
Rib	Narrow gold tinsel.
Hackle	Coch-y-bonddu all the way up.
Shoulder	Gallina.
Wings	Slices of brown speckled turkey, but a shade darker than before, and with an under wing of peacock breast feather.
Head	Black.
Hooks	6–8

No. 4

Tag	Gold tinsel.
Tail	A few fibres of tippet and black partridge.
Body	Light yellow (almost lemon) floss.
Rib	Narrow gold tinsel.
Hackle	Red (almost cinnamon) all the way up.
Shoulder	Gallina.
Wings	An under wing of tippet sprigs with brown speckled turkey over.
Head	Black.
Hook	7

Mr Parker who lives at Halton also sent me some Lune patterns with which he had done very well.

No. 1

Tag	Gold tinsel and bright red floss.
Tail	A topping.
Body	Dark blue floss.
Rib	Gold thread.
Hackle	Jay all the way up.

Mr Parker's No. 1

Shoulder A rich dark violet hackle.
Wings Sprigs of gallina, red and blue macaw, and the speckled brown feather from a pea-hen's back.
Head Black.
Hooks 6–8

No. 2
Tag Gold tinsel.
Tail A topping.
Body Light blue floss.
Rib Gold thread.
Hackle Black all the way up.
Shoulder Gallina.
Wings Slices of dun turkey with lightish tips, and a few sprigs of tippet, red parrot, florican bustard, and wood-duck.
Head Black.
Hooks 6–8

THE RIBBLE AND HODDER

This with its important tributaries would be a splendid river if it was only given a chance; but with pollution from the mills, and haaf, wholesale and other nets it is sorely entreated.
Mr Pritt, who until very recently concerned himself very much in the affairs of the river, sends me the following.

The Ramsbottom's Parson *Colour plate 8*
This is a fly of strong contrasts and is dressed without a tag, butt, and body hackle.
Tail Two bright yellow hackle points.
Body Medium yellow wool rough and picked out.
Rib Silver tinsel.
Shoulder A cobalt blue hackle.
Wings Five or six bright yellow hackles with black centres; over them two bright red-claret hackles.
Head Black.
Hook 6

The Yellow and Scarlet Mallard
Tag Gold twist and gold-coloured floss.
Tail Slips of red, and yellow swan with a kingfisher feather.
Butt Black ostrich herl.
Body Mixed orange, yellow, and scarlet wool, rough and picked out.
Rib Fine gold twist.
Hackle None.
Shoulder An orange-yellow hackle with jay over it.
Wings Slips of red, purple, and lemon swan, with slices of brown mallard over.
Head Black.
Hook 6

The Green Mallard *Colour plate 8*
Tag Gold twist and ruby floss.
Tail Sprigs of tippet and green parrot.
Butt Black ostrich herl.
Body Golden-green floss the shade of a beetle's wing.
Rib Gold thread.
Hackle Reddish claret all the way up.
Shoulder Blue jay.
Wings Under wing, sprigs of tippet and pale green swan. Over wing, a little bit of claret-red swan, a few golden pheasant tail sprigs and slices of brown mallard.
Head Black.
Hook 6

I also had three patterns from Mr Ramsbottom of Clitheroe who is the great fly-tying authority on the river. The first was his Parson, already described, along with the following two others.

The Cinnamon
This one has no tag, butt or body hackle.
Tail Two red hackle points, something between lake and scarlet.
Body Pig's wool, the same colour as the tail.
Rib Broad silver tinsel.
Shoulder A hackle the same colour as the tail and body. (No body hackle.)

Wings	Three hackles of the same colour red (in the middle), and cinnamon red hackles on either side.
Head	Black.
Hook	6

The Winesop Black *Colour plate 8*

Mr Ramsbottom says this is a 'real old Ribble favourite'. It has no tag or butt.

Tag	A few shreds of orange mohair with two or three red ones thrown in.
Body	Bright lake floss.
Rib	Narrow silver tinsel.
Hackle	Darkish medium blue all the way up.
Shoulder	Darkish medium blue same as the hackle.
Wings	Two slips of mottled silver-grey turkey or peacock.
Head	Black.
Hook	6

THE TYNE

At one time the Tyne gave promise of being one of the best salmon rivers in the kingdom; but the nets multiplied, grew, and combined so that the river has nearly returned again to its wonted state.

Mr Cook, of Hexham, has sent me three patterns which he states are not to be beaten.

No. 1

Tag	Silver twist and gold floss.
Tail	A bit of tippet.
Butt	Black ostrich herl.
Body	Gold thread.
Rib	None.

The Cinnamon

Hackle	Two hackles are employed, a deep orange and a yellow are run on together, all the way up the body.
Shoulder	Medium blue with teal over.
Wings	Two shortish toppings and a saddle feather from a golden pheasant with sprigs of blue, and claret swan, some tippet and grey drake, a little golden pheasant tail, a bit of peacock wing and another topping over all.
Cheeks	Short jungle-cock.
Head	Black.
Hook	6

A very elaborate fly.

No. 2 *Colour plate 8*

Tag	Gold tinsel.
Tail	A topping with sprigs of tippet, red, yellow, and blue swan.
Butt	Black ostrich herl.
Body	Of wool, starting with yellow, merging into a warm medium red.
Rib	Fine gold tinsel.
Hackle	Golden olive.
Shoulder	Jay.
Wings	Mixed fibres of brown mallard, tippet, violet, red, yellow, and green swan.
Head	Black.
Hook	8

No. 3

Tag	Gold tinsel.
Tail	A shred of tippet.
Butt	None.
Body	Magenta wool.
Rib	Narrow gold tinsel.
Hackle	Of a shade between magenta and claret.
Shoulder	Black.
Wings	Two coch-y-bonddu hackles, with brown mallard on either side.
Head	Black.
Hook	9

Mr Robson, of Hexham, sent me the pattern of his pet fly which is very good for the Beaufront water.

Tag	Silver tinsel and medium blue floss.
Tail	A sprig of teal.
Butt	Black ostrich herl.
Body	Two turns of golden floss, the rest of purple claret pig's wool.
Rib	Silver tinsel.
Hackle	None.
Shoulder	An orange hackle with gallina over.
Wings	Brown mallard and teal.
Cheeks	Short jungle-cock.
Head	Black.
Hook	8

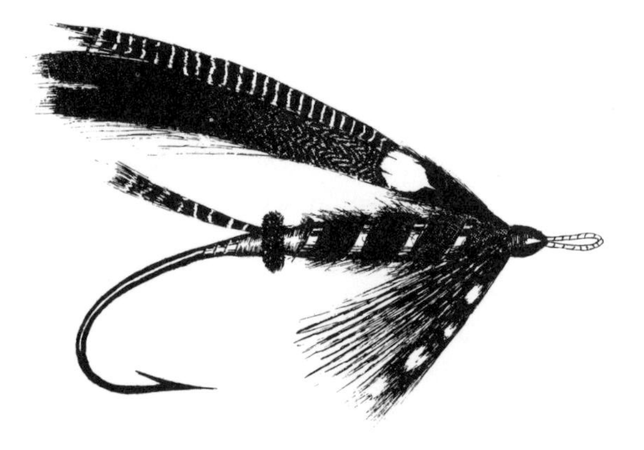

Mr Robson's pattern

THE TAW AND TORRIDGE

These patterns are from Farlow's.

No. 1

Tag	Silver tinsel.
Tail	A topping and red and blue macaw.
Butt	Black ostrich herl.
Body	Three turns of medium orange floss, the rest of darkish blue pig's wool.
Rib	Broad silver tinsel.
Hackle	Medium blue.
Shoulder	Blue jay.
Wings	A darkish blue hackle, then slices of brick-red swan and dark grey speckled turkey.
Head	Black.
Hooks	5–9

No. 2 *Colour plate 8*

Tag	Silver thread and ruby floss.
Tail	A topping.
Butt	Black ostrich herl.
Body	Pale yellow wool.
Rib	Silver tinsel.
Hackle	Light orange.
Shoulder	A light orange hackle inclining to pale brick-red.
Wings	Brown speckled turkey, peacock, a few sprigs of florican bustard, and grey mallard slightly brown at the tips over all.
Head	Black.
Hooks	5–9

No. 3

Tag	Gold tinsel.
Tail	A topping.
Butt	Black ostrich herl.
Body	Bright canary-coloured floss.
Rib	Gold tinsel.
Hackle	Bright canary-coloured to match the body.
Shoulder	Blue jay.
Wings	Mixed sprigs of bustard, tippet, wood-duck, gallina, and a topping over all.

Horns	Blue macaw.
Head	Black.
Hooks	5–9

In the early spring, a Butcher dressed smallish is a first-rate fly for these rivers.

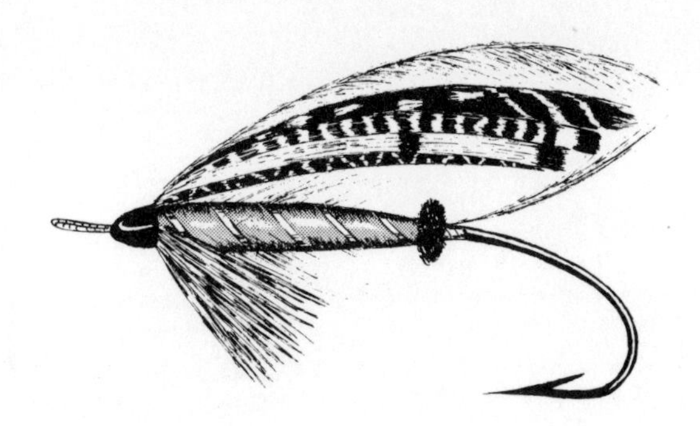

Mr Farlow's No. 3

Appendix A

How to Dress a Salmon Fly

It is unlikely that the expert will have any problems in following the patterns given within the pages of this book, which primarily is a book of traditional salmon fly patterns. However, it would surely be unreasonable, if not unkind, for the novice to possess such an array of beautiful patterns without being given some indication of how to set about tying them. So, especially for the new-comers to the fascinating art of fly-tying, and for those whose experience has so far been limited to tying trout flies, I have included this appendix.

A good point to bear in mind when tying salmon flies is that there are no hard and fast rules. The reason is simple – what you are creating is not intended to represent a particular fly; it is a lure designed to arouse the curiosity of a creature which has no real desire to feed once it has entered into fresh water from the sea. Therefore, do not attempt to follow patterns as though they were law, but rather, as in any form of art, which fly tying undoubtedly is, I would encourage you to be inventive and develop your own style and techniques, and ultimately your own patterns. I have simply attempted here to give you some basic guidelines which I hope you will find helpful, and have avoided as much as possible any complicated instructions. However, for those wishing to study the tying of salmon flies in greater depth I cannot do better than recommend to you that superb book by T. E. Pryce-Tannett, *How to Dress Salmon Flies*, a delightfully informative work which is also published by Adam & Charles Black.

In tying flies from description it is usual that instructions for covering the shank of the hook will begin at the point nearest the bend. In the majority of patterns the first part will be the Tag which is followed by the Tail, then the Butt, the Body, the Rib, the Hackle (body), and the Shoulder. By studying 'The Parts of a Salmon Fly' on page xii you will get an idea what these parts look like. The wings in many patterns are sometimes fairly complicated in design, but in most fully dressed salmon flies instructions will begin with the Under Wing (where one is included), followed by the Over Wing which will often include a golden pheasant crest feather, more commonly referred to as a *topping*, sitting over the wings. Then (when these parts are included) comes the Cheeks, then the Horns, and lastly the Head to complete the fly.

Hooks

Salmon fly hooks, often referred to as salmon irons, should be of the best quality steel wire with a smooth coating of black lacquer – although why it should have to be black is a mystery. Only buy the best, the tip being, 'yer get what yer pays for'. As for design, there is possibly none better than the Limerick hook, although a good many tyers have a preference for Sproat or Dee type hooks. However, I am sure that they each hook fish equally well. Hooks with ready made eyes were difficult to purchase in Francis Francis' days, which is why old salmon flies are often found with an eye of looped gut which tyers would first bind to the shank prior to dressing the fly. Such eyes will be

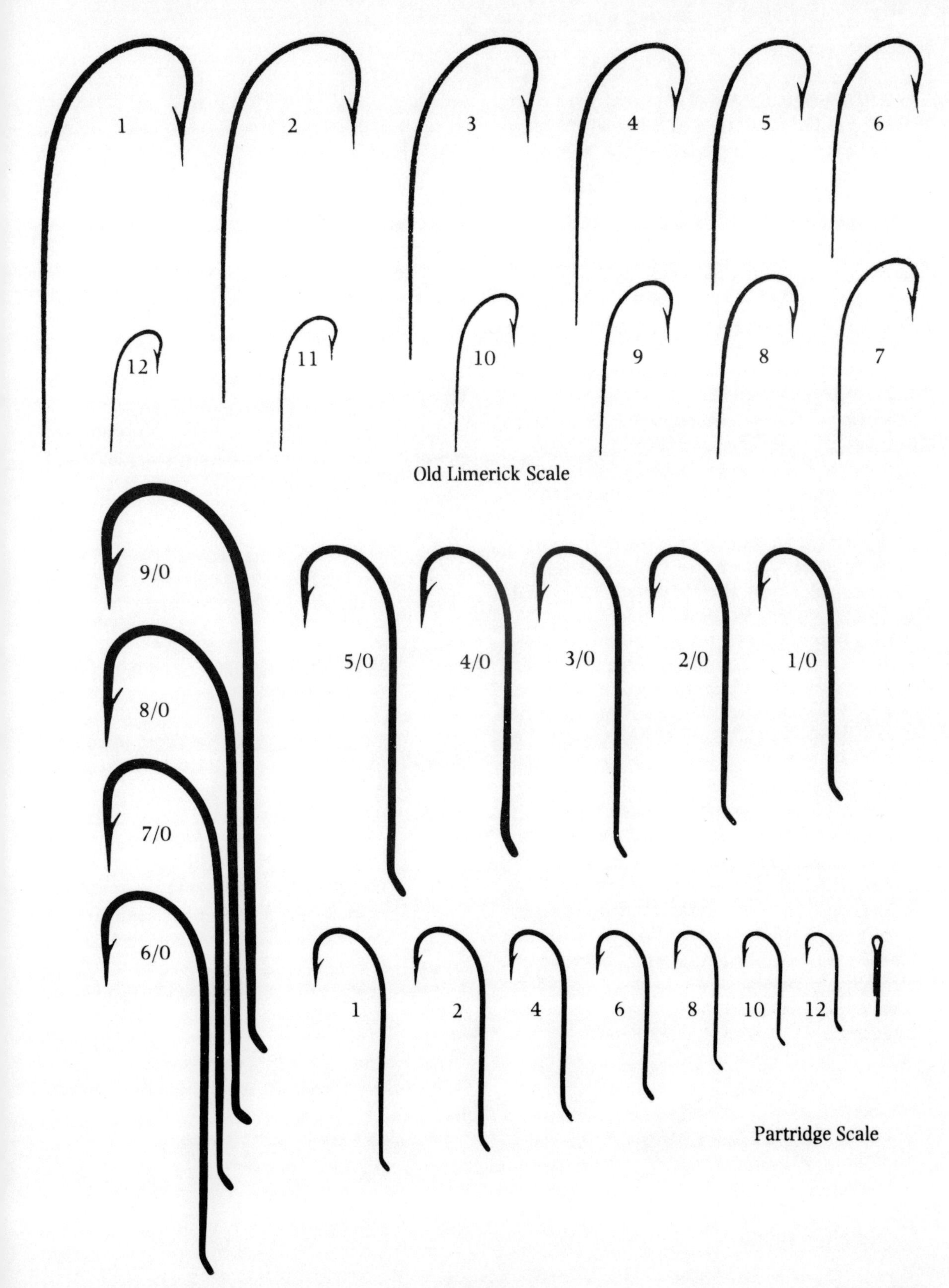
1
2
3
4
5
6
12
11
10
9
8
7
Old Limerick Scale
9/0
8/0
7/0
6/0
5/0
4/0
3/0
2/0
1/0
1
2
4
6
8
10
12
Partridge Scale

HOOK SIZE

seen in the drawings which illustrate some of the patterns in this book. However, in modern hooks this problem no longer exists, which is why the illustrations in this appendix are shown with the more familiar upturned looped eye.

Francis Francis complained that hook scales varied so much between one manufacturer and another. I am afraid that today, over 100 years later, the situation remains much the same, and hook manufacturers still seem unable to reach a common consensus on sizes. The best I am able to do is to give you the scale used by that world famous manufacturer of hooks, Partridge of Redditch, which is shown on page 87 and which you may wish to compare with the old Limerick scale in the same illustration. You will note that Partridge make hooks up to size 9/0 and in fact many of the old traditional patterns were dressed on such large hooks. Also, for those who would prefer to dress flies in the traditional fashion, Partridge will supply the old style salmon hooks without eyes in size 2/0.

As for bends, there may be a fair number of styles to choose from, but basically all salmon fly hooks fall into two types, these being the standard hook on which the fully dressed fly is tied, and which is more suited for spring fishing in heavy water. The second type is the low-water hook which is made from a finer gauge wire and designed for dressing a lighter fly for use in summer conditions when the river is low and when fish can be taken close to the surface. Almost any pattern can have its low-water counterpart by dressing the fly sparse, using the minimum amount of materials. They also seem to fish more effectively, at least in my own experience, if they are dressed with a short body – short, that is, in comparison to the length of the hook. Low-water hooks rarely exceed size 1 in the Partridge scale as salmon more usually prefer a smaller fly in the summer months. The general guide is, the higher the water, the larger the fly. But salmon fishing is a peculiar game and full of exceptions to the rule. A few years ago I took a very large fish on the River Ribble on a size 5/0 (Partridge) Jock Scott in dead low conditions after having fished unsuccessfully all day with small flies. Perhaps this goes to show that there is nothing more conducive to sport when it is slack than a radical change in method.

Low-water type pattern

Tying a Fly

To help you gain at least some fundamental skill in tying a salmon fly, I have included one of my own patterns which is a relatively easy one to dress and one which contains most of the parts which you are likely to encounter when tying any of the Francis Francis collection. I will explain the particular use of the tools of the trade as I take you stage by stage through the process of dressing a fly from the pattern which I give you below.

Tag	Silver tinsel and yellow floss.
Tail	A topping and some tippet feather fibres.
Butt	Black ostrich herl.
Body	Black silk floss.
Rib	Silver tinsel to suit the size of the fly.
Hackle	Black, starting about one-quarter way up.
Shoulder	Black (cock hackle).
Wings	An Under Wing of two golden pheasant tippet feathers, back to back (as in the Rangers). The Over Wing is a mixed one with 'married' fibres of golden pheasant tail, blue, yellow, and red swan, and a topping over all.
Cheeks	Kingfisher, or similar dyed feather.
Horns	Blue macaw.
Head	Black.
Hooks	1 to 5/0 (Partridge scale).

And without further ado we will proceed to tie our fly.

The first, and obvious, thing to do is to fix your hook in the vice which should be a strong one with jaws wide enough to hold a larger hook firmly in place, and presuming that you are right-handed (my apologies to left-handed tyers) the eye of the hook should point to your right. Now insert a bobbin of black tying silk in your bobbin holder and thread the end through the narrow spout. Tying silks should always match the colour of the fly's body, which is my reason for specifying black in this case. Starting at the eye of the hook, wind on in neat and close turns a bed of tying silk in a clockwise direction to a point about level with the point of the barb. When this is done apply a drop of clear varnish over the silk, using the point of your dubbing needle. This will help to hold the tying silk firmly in place and prevent it from turning when tying in the rest of the body. Now you are ready to tie in the first part of your fly, which is the Tag.

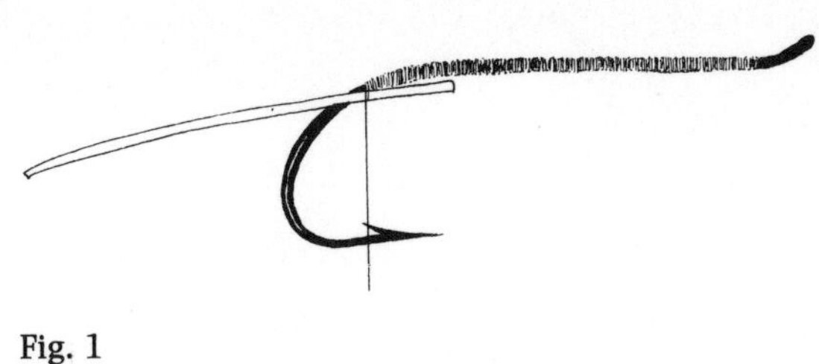

Fig. 1

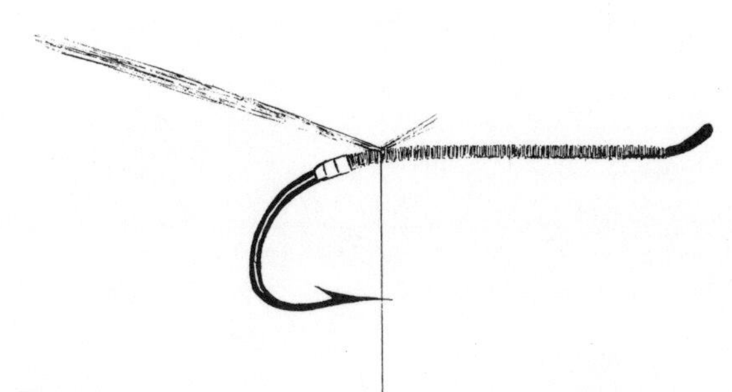

Fig. 2

The Tag

Tie in a few inches of narrow silver tinsel on the underside of the shank in the position shown in Fig. 1. The tinsel will form the first part of the tag, which is sometimes called the *tip.* Now hold the loose end of the tinsel in your hackle pliers and wind on three or four tight turns back towards the eye in an anti-clockwise direction, making sure that the turns fit flush up to each other. When you have done this tie in the tinsel and cut off the surplus. Now at a point a little way above the turns of tinsel tie in about 10 in. of the yellow floss (see Fig. 2) which will be used to form the second part of the tag. Wind the floss in an anti-clockwise direction down towards the turns of tinsel, overlapping it slightly, and back again to the point where you began. On the way back the turns should overlap a little so that the tag becomes wider as it progresses towards the eye. (See Fig. 3.) Because the fibres of floss silk separate easily this is best done with the fingers, rather than holding the end of the floss with the hackle pliers.

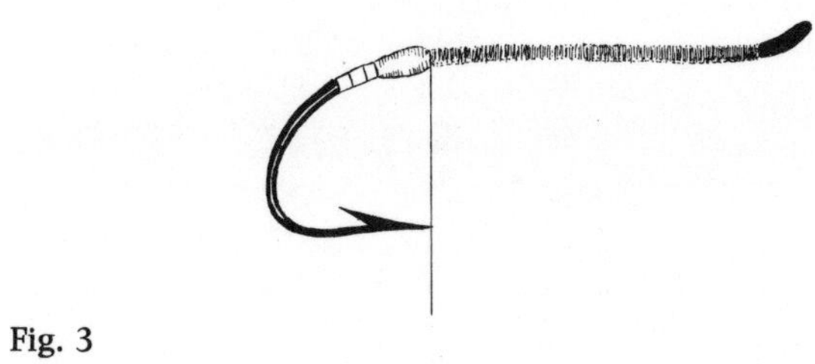

Fig. 3

The Tail

Tie in a few fibres from a golden pheasant tippet feather and a topping to turn upwards, roughly matching the bend of the hook opposite. (See Fig. 4.)

Fig. 4

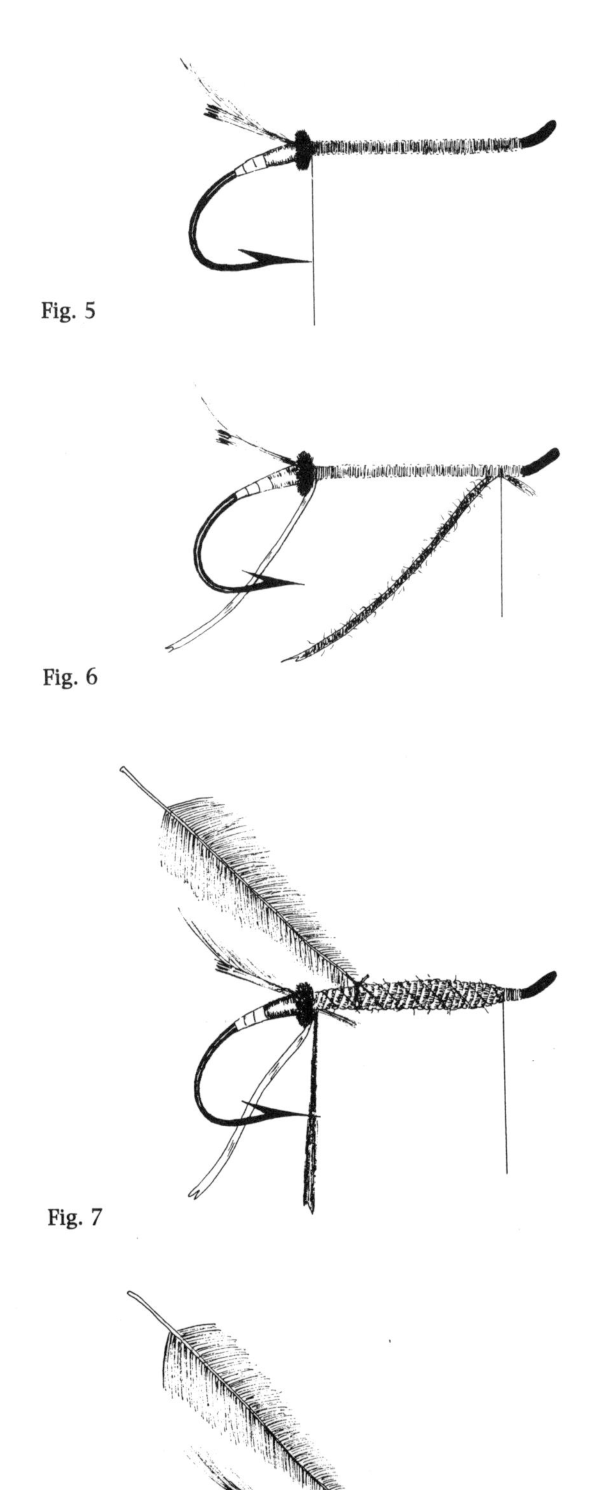
Fig. 5

Fig. 6

Fig. 7

Fig. 8

The Butt

From a black ostrich plume select a herl which should be as long and wide as possible and tie it in, again as shown in Fig. 4. Hold the end of the herl in your hackle pliers and wind on the herl in an anti-clockwise direction to form the butt (see Fig. 5). You will have to be extremely careful in doing this as ostrich herls tend to snap quite easily. To obtain a good-looking butt may require some practice but if, when winding on, you ensure that the tiny fibres are pointing backwards, and you are careful not to overlap the turns, then you should not have too many problems. When you think the butt looks about right tie it in and cut off the surplus herl.

The Body

Before you actually begin to dress the body, tie in about 4 in. of silver tinsel close to the butt (see Fig. 6); this will later be wound over the body to form the rib. Now take the tying silk back to a point a little short of the eye and tie in about 18 in. of fine black wool, as again shown in Fig. 6. Wind the wool in close even turns up to the butt and back again towards the eye. While returning the wool, overlap slightly around the shoulder area to give the body a realistic looking shape. Tie in the wool at the point where you began and remove the surplus. Now wind the tying silk over the wool to the butt. On reaching the butt tie in about 18 in. of the black silk floss (see Fig. 7) then wind the silk back towards the eye and at a point roughly one quarter up the length of the body, tie in a black cock hackle at its point for the body hackle (see Fig. 7) and continue winding the silk back towards the eye. Again, as when winding on the floss for the tag, use your fingers to wind on the black floss towards the eye in an anti-clockwise direction, covering the wool in close even turns. Tie in and cut off the surplus. Your fly should now resemble Fig. 8.

The Rib

Holding the end of the tinsel in the hackle pliers, wind on the ribbing in open spirals back to the eye in a clockwise direction. The distance between each spiral depends on the size of the fly you are tying and on how 'flashy' you want the fly to appear. A fly with plenty of flash about it will, for instance, kill better on a bright day and a duller fly on a dull day. Consequently, you may wish to produce more than one version of the same fly. However, my own version of this particular fly would have about five or six turns to it. In smaller flies narrow tinsel is used – the rule being the larger the fly, the wider the tinsel. When you have wound on the ribbing tie it in and remove the surplus. (See Fig. 9.)

Fig. 9

The Hackle

The hackle, or rather the *body* hackle, should come from a cock bird and be of the finest quality with a brilliant translucency. Before winding it on a little preparation is necessary so that it will lie with the fibres pointing backwards. Take the butt of the hackle between the forefinger and thumb of your right hand (or with the hackle pliers if the hackle is a small one) and hold it vertical. Then using the forefinger and thumb of your left hand stroke the fibres to the left (see Fig. 10), ensuring that the best

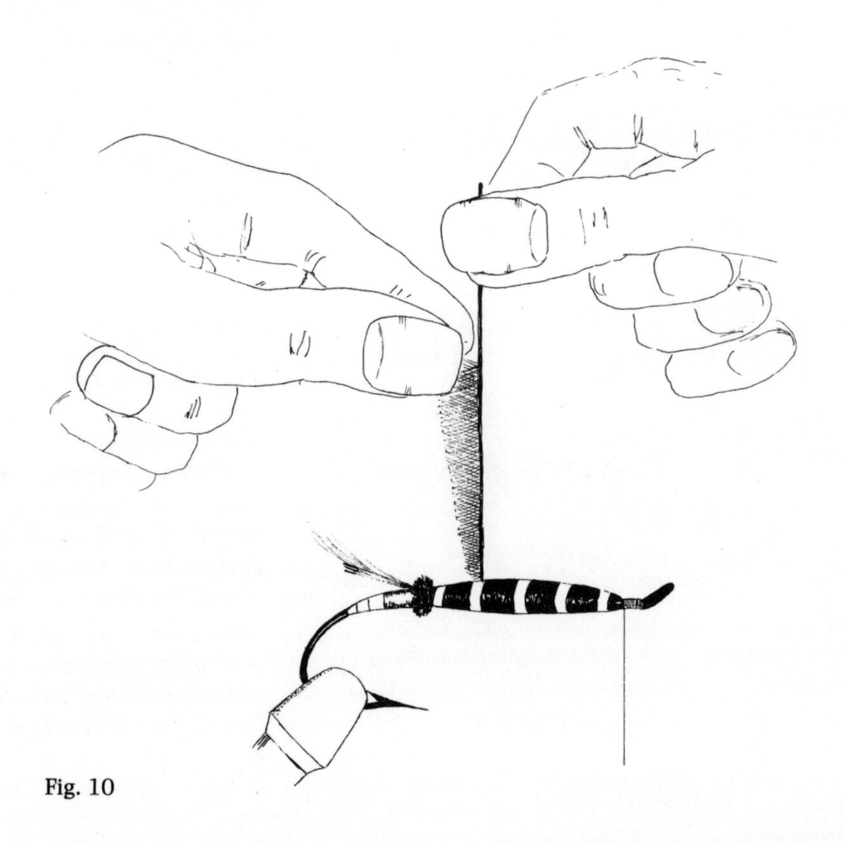

Fig. 10

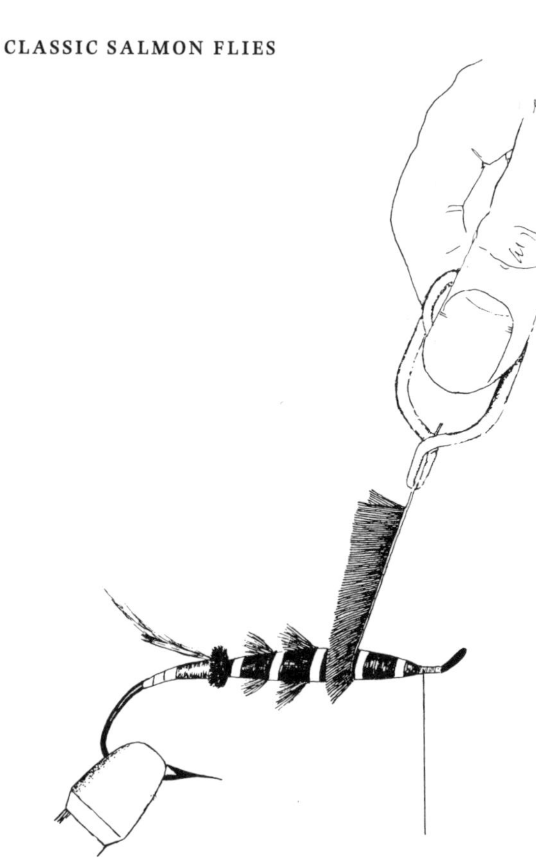

Fig. 11

side of the feather is on the outside, until a 'V' sectional appearance is achieved. This process is known as 'doubling', but I should ask you to take care in doing this so that you do not pull the hackle free of the body. Now hold the butt of the hackle in the hackle pliers and wind it round the body, following tight up behind each spiral of the rib (see Fig. 11). When you have reached the point just short of the eye, tie the hackle in tight and cut off the surplus quill. You are now at the stage shown in Fig. 12.

Here is an alternative method which, although a little more difficult, will give your fly that professional touch. The procedure is to wind on the hackle before winding on the floss. Using this method there will be no need to double the fibres as before. Wind the hackle over the wool in fairly close turns, then wind on the floss allowing the hackle fibres to protrude between each turn. While winding on the floss, stroke the hackle fibres backwards and allow the turns of the floss to hold them in place. Other fibres which might get caught up in the turns of floss can be picked out with the point of your dubbing needle.

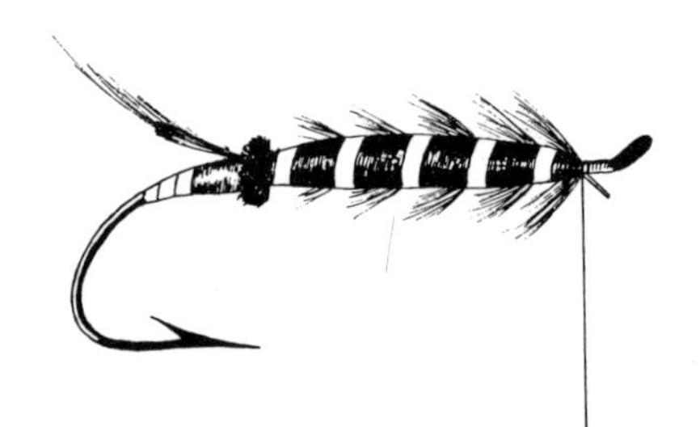

Fig. 12

The Shoulder

The black hackle which we will use for the shoulder will be of equal quality to the one used for the body hackle and will again be from a cock, except that this time the hackle will be longer in the fibres. How much longer is a matter of taste; some tyers like the points of the shoulder fibres to reach the point of the hook, while others tie them short. A fly will look most acceptable if the fibre points end somewhere level with the middle of the body once they are tied in in their natural position, except, that is, for patterns which call for longer fibres. I often prefer to prepare hackles for the shoulder by first stripping all the fibres from the left-hand side of the quill. By left-hand I mean the left-hand side of the feather when looking at its best side while it is pointing vertical. By preparing the hackle in this way it will not only be easier to wind on, but will prevent it from taking up too much space in the very limited section between the end of the body and the eye. Tying in a full hackle in this space could cause us problems when we come to tie in the wings and form the head and as there is obviously much to do in this short space we need to avoid letting the dressing encroach too closely to the eye at this stage.

Unlike the body hackle, the shoulder hackle is tied in at its butt. The best way to start is to hold it at an angle behind the hook before binding on with a few tight turns of the silk. (See Fig. 13). Now hold the point of the hackle in your hackle pliers and with the forefinger and thumb of your left hand pull the fibres to stand straight out at a right-angle from the quill. Wind on five or six turns in an anti-clockwise direction, tie in and cut off the surplus to produce Fig. 14. Now separate the fibres equally on either side of the hook and with the forefinger and thumb of your left hand pull them down and towards the point of the hook. We now have to secure the fibres in this position, which is easily achieved by taking one or two turns of the silk back over the fibres at an angle as shown in Fig. 15 and

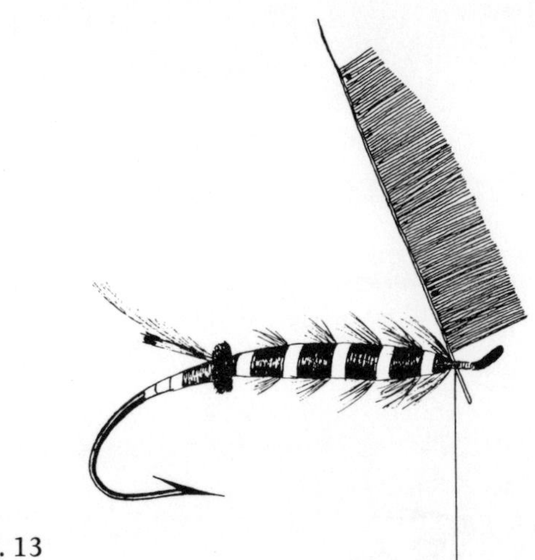

Fig. 13

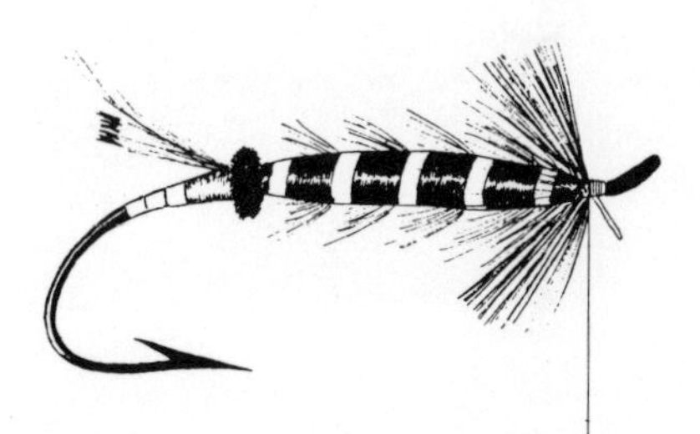

Fig. 14

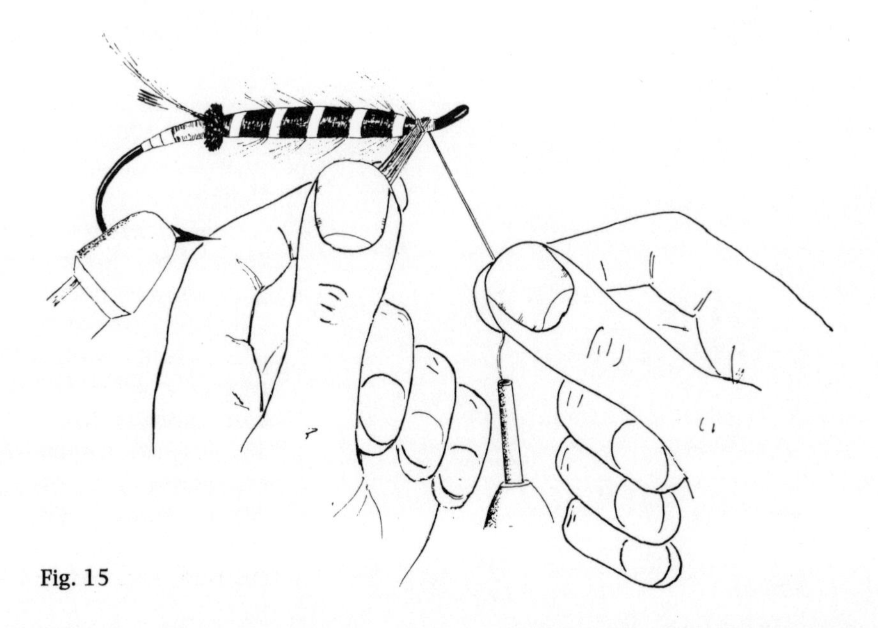

Fig. 15

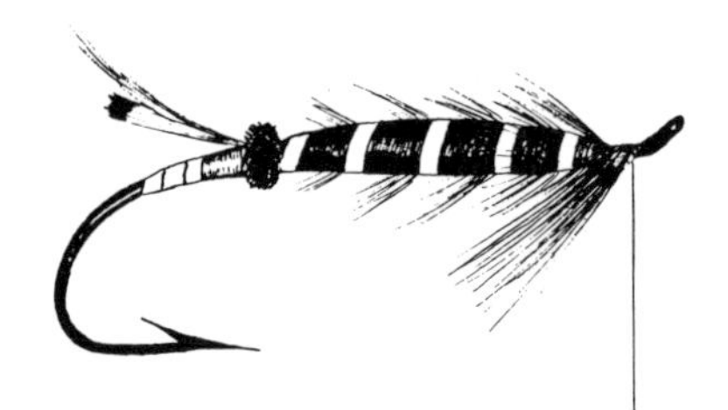

Fig. 16

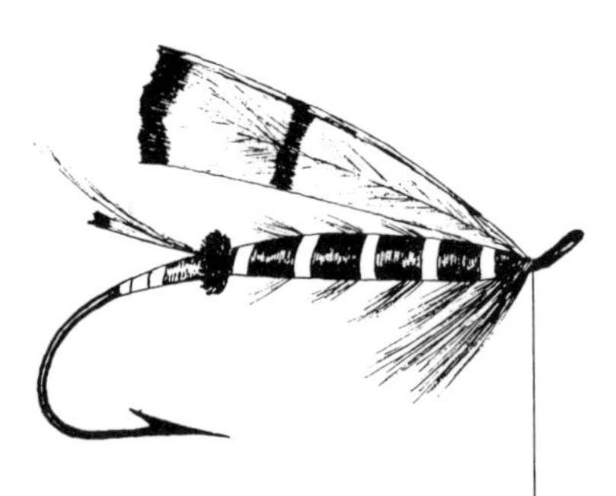

Fig. 17

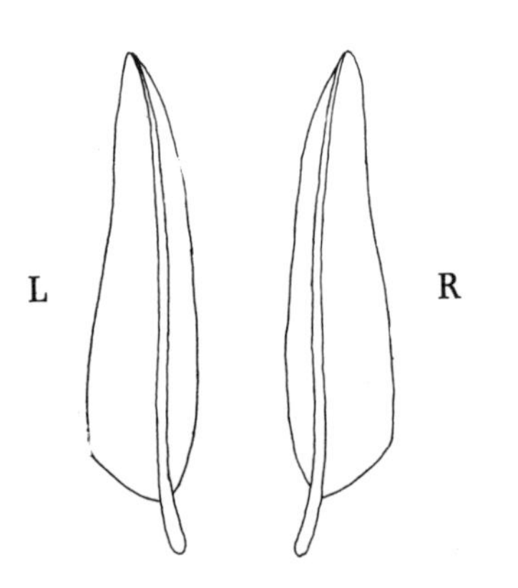

Fig. 18

completed in Fig. 16. You may have to make a few minor adjustments before the shoulder looks just right, but once it is, apply a drop of clear varnish over the turns of tying silk with the point of your dubbing needle to help hold it firmer in place while the wings are being tied in.

An alternative method known as a 'false beard' can be used if preferred, and indeed a good many tyers use no other method. Instead of winding on a hackle, simply tie in a bunch of fibres under the throat of the fly to achieve the same effect. This is a very simple operation which can cut out much work and time.

The Wings

A good many traditional patterns include an Under Wing which is usually of tippet feathers or turkey tail. It is best described as a *base wing* over which the main wing, or Over Wing, is positioned, but to my mind the Under Wing (or inner wing) is a luxury which in many flies could be dispensed with. I have given it here for no other reason than the fact that so many patterns seem to include them.

Select two matching tippet feathers which should be long enough to reach as far as the Tag, once tied in. Remove the white fluffy feathers from around the roots and tie them in back to back to produce Fig. 17. It will be found easier to tie the tippets in if you first press your thumb nail into the quills at the point where they are to be tied in. It may also help to keep the tippets together while tying them in if you first wet the forefinger and thumb of your left hand and then gently draw the feathers through them while held together.

Now comes the Over Wing of mixed, or 'married' fibres. This perhaps is the most difficult and intricate operation in producing a salmon fly. My only advice here is if at first you don't get it right, don't give up. With a little practice you will soon become an expert at this and capable of making the finest married wings without too much difficulty. The majority of salmon fly wings are built up from an assortment of dyed and natural feathers which are 'married' together. The fibres for the right-hand wing, which is the one nearest to you when the hook is in the vice, are taken from the right-hand side of the feathers. You will therefore be correct in assuming that the fibres for the left-hand wing will come from the left-hand side of the feathers. (See Fig. 18.) The ideal feathers will, of course, be the matching pair from the opposite sides of the same bird, and, in fact, this is how they are sold. A number of feathers have fibres of equal length on either side of the quill, which means that the same feather can be used for the production of both wings.

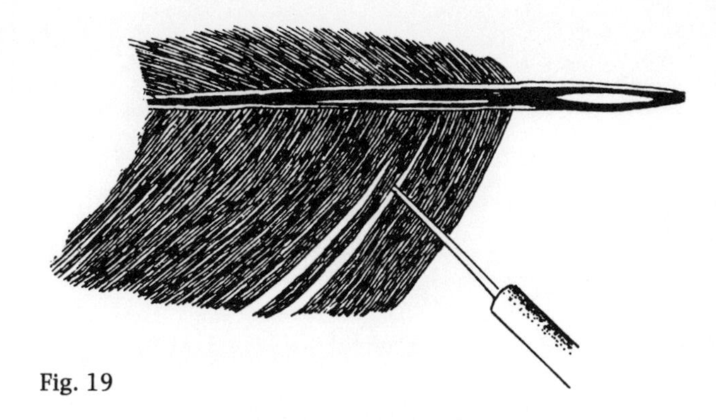

Fig. 19

Let us first construct the left-hand wing and begin by removing a section of fibres from the left-hand side of a golden pheasant tail. This is easily done by separating the fibres you intend to use with the point of your dubbing needle. (See Fig. 19.) All you then have to do is lift the separated section and snip it off close to the quill. Next, select fibres of a similar width and length from the left-hand side of the blue swan feather. We now have to take advantage of nature's natural way of holding the fibres of a feather in place. Along the edge of each separate fibre is a series of tiny claw-like hairs which grip their opposite numbers to hold them in place in a similar way to that of a zip

Fig. 20

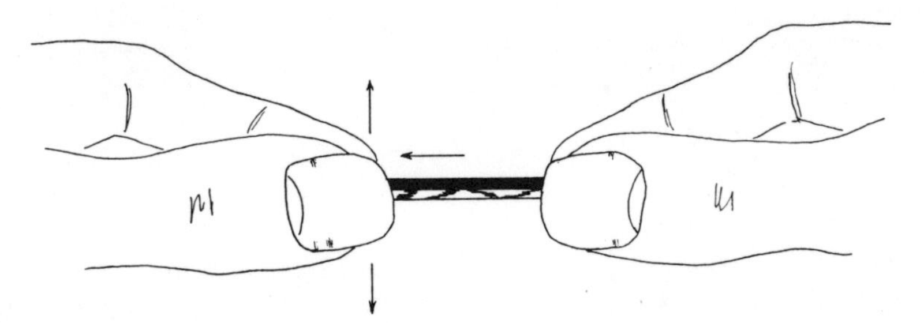

Fig. 21

fastener. (See Fig. 20.) By understanding how this works the task of 'marrying' wing sections is made easier. Place the blue swan fibres over the golden pheasant tail fibres with the tip of the swan slightly extending. Grip the butts of the fibres between the forefinger and thumb of your right hand and the extreme tips of the fibres between the forefinger and thumb of your left hand. Now pull the fibres gently to the left while at the same time moving the tips slightly up and down. (See Fig. 21.). This will cause the claws to interlock (see Fig. 22), and

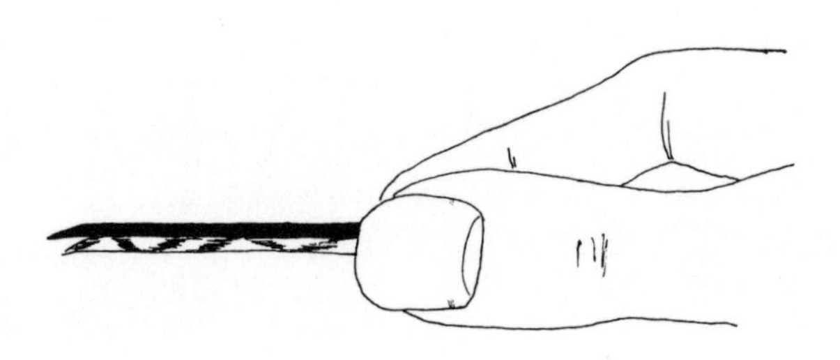

Fig. 22

Fig. 23

when the fibres become held together, repeat the process with the yellow swan, and again with the red swan to complete the left-hand wing. All you have to do now is to build the right wing using fibres from the right-hand feathers. To build a good wing you should remember that each time a new section is added it should slightly extend the one below it. (See Fig. 23.) Also, make sure that left-hand sections do not get mixed up with right-hand ones as they will not marry up well and will cause the wing to split when you come to tie it in.

Tying in wings of any kind can be a tricky operation, but tying in 'married' wings will require an additional amount of skill and concentration, as it is at this stage that the risk of the wings splitting is a real one. You would find it useful to first practice with whole sections taken from feathers. Because our fly has an Under Wing, the job becomes even more difficult, because instead of tying in the wings back to back in the usual way, the procedure is to tie them in on either side of the tippet feathers. This is a method known as 'veiling', and what we are about to do is veil the Over Wing over the upper half of the Under Wing.

To tie them in, hold the married wings firmly in position on either side of the tippet feathers, using the forefinger and thumb of your left hand as shown in Fig. 24(a). At the point of tying in, the butts of the wings should be touching together immediately above the body, and below the eye, on top of the tied in roots of the tippet feathers, and should be as near as possible to the position shown in Fig. 24(a). Tie in by taking the silk up between the nearside wing and the thumb, then down again between the far wing and forefinger, forming a loop over the top of the wings as shown in Fig. 24(b). The art is to keep a firm enough grip while doing this, thus preventing the wings from being pulled out of position. With the silk and wings held firmly between the forefinger and thumb, pull the silk down fairly tight so that the fibres are compressed together against the hook as in Fig. 25(a). While pulling the silk tight, your grip should be slackened ever so slightly to allow the fibres to compress. However, please take care not to slacken your grip too much or this will result in the fibres being bent over instead of compressing neatly on

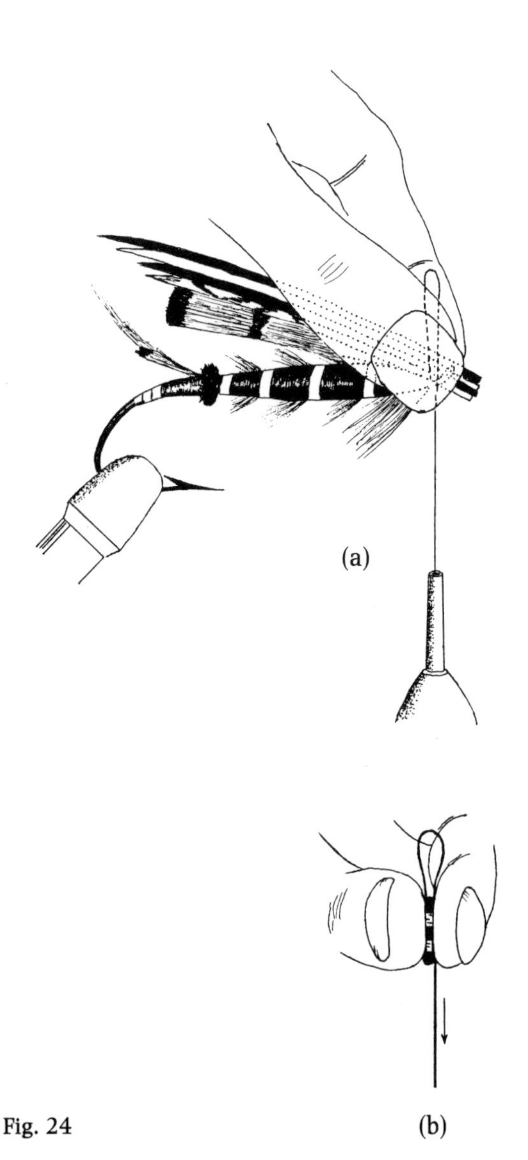

Fig. 24

top of each other, and will cause the wings to split. (See Fig. 25(b).) Your fly should now resemble Fig. 26. Remember also to make use of your tweezers when picking up wings, or parts of wings, rather than risk splitting them with your fingers.

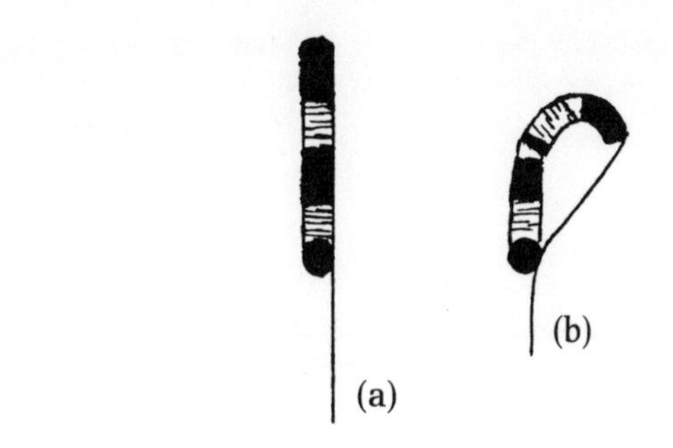

Fig. 25

The Topping

The topping is a golden pheasant crest feather which sits neatly over the top of the wings, adding that certain 'finished' look to the fly with its brilliant golden fibres.

Select a crest feather which is a little longer than the wings and remove the unwanted fluffy fibres from around the root. It will help to tie it in if you first press your thumb nail into the stem of the feather as shown in Fig. 27(a). This will cause the stem to bend upwards as in Fig. 27(b) and by holding the bent up part over the head part of the fly (see Fig. 28) it will make the job of tying it in an easy one and will also assist in positioning it correctly over the wings.

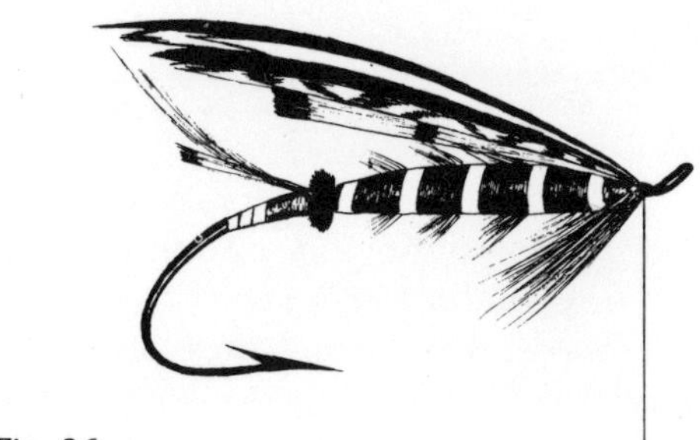
Fig. 26

The Cheeks

Some tyers never bother to include cheeks, but in my own opinion, a fly without cheeks is like a birthday cake without candles; they serve to enhance the fly's attraction and add extra sparkle to the wings. In some flies jungle-cock is used, but in the best interest of conservation jungle-cock is now very difficult to obtain. However, substitutes for these beautiful, enamelled-eyed feathers can be easily produced by applying dabs of white and orange Humbrol paint to black hen hackles. Alternatively, substitutes can be purchased but these can be very expensive. Blue chatterer was once an important feather used in the cheeks, but again these too are now very rare and have been replaced by kingfisher, which is the feather used in our pattern.

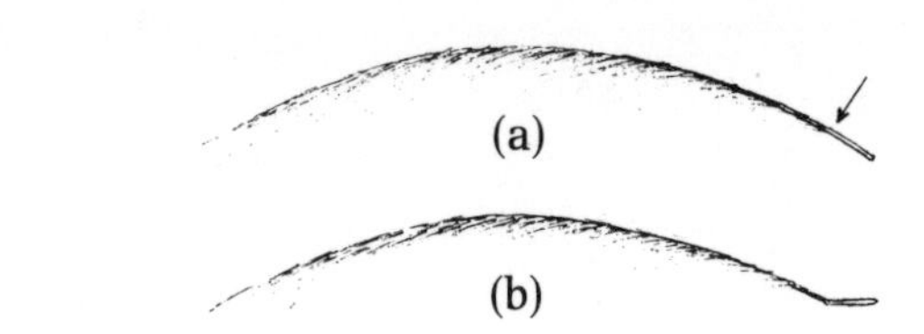

Fig. 27

Select two similar sized feathers from the back of a kingfisher and tie them in, one either side of the wings. You may have some trouble in keeping these small feathers in position while tying them in; therefore you might find it easier to wet them first and tie them in while they are still adhered to the sides of the wings.

Many patterns have in them *sides*, which are not

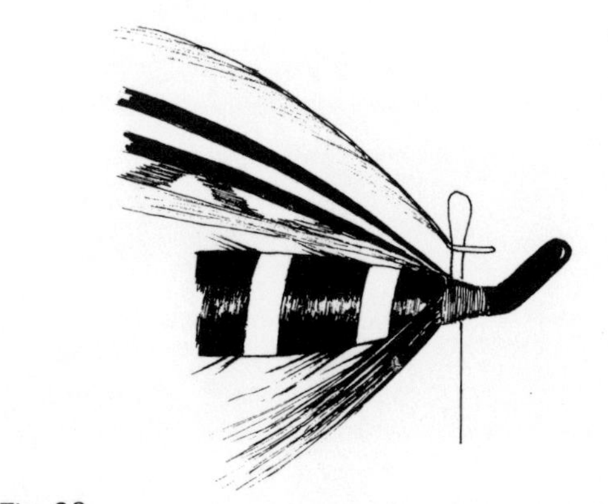
Fig. 28

to be confused with cheeks. Sides are simply feathers which are tied in over the finished wings and are usually of the same length as the wings, unlike the shorter feathers used in cheeks.

The Horns
The horns are two long single fibres of blue macaw which are meant to represent the antennae of a large insect or moth. They originate from very early days when it was believed that the salmon took the fly for a butterfly or some similar creature. As blue macaw is now difficult to obtain, horns are rarely incorporated and you may be forgiven for omitting this part of the fly. However, if you are able to obtain some blue macaw, then tie in two single fibres to sweep back over the wings.

The Head
To complete the fly, wind on enough turns of silk as is necessary to form a nice looking head. Finish with a couple of half hitches or a whip finish and cut off the silk. If you have tied the fly correctly then at no time will the black tying silk have been cut until you have finished off at the head. Now dab onto the head a drop of clear varnish and allow it to soak into the tying silk and, once it has dried, finish the head with a coat of black varnish.

How to Dress a Dubbing Body

Many of the flies in this book are dressed with bodies of pig's fur. This material, though, is no longer readily available and today such bodies are dressed with seal's fur which I consider a far better material. The fur is applied to the body by a method known as 'dubbing' which is quite a simple undertaking. Dubbing on a fur body should commence at the tail of the fly. Start by pulling the tying silk taut, then dip your dubbing needle into the liquid wax and with it run a coating of the wax over a few inches of the tying silk. Whilst holding the tying silk taut with your left hand, take a small pinch of seal's fur between the forefinger and thumb of your right hand and roll it on to the tying silk in a clockwise direction, while spreading the fur in even proportion along the silk. The fur will attach itself easily to the silk owing to the tackiness of liquid wax. Keep repeating this procedure until you have enough fur attached to the silk to cover the body (or joint of the body) when wound on. The fur can later be picked out with the point of the dubbing needle to give the body a rough or bushy appearance.

Appendix B

Feathers and Substitutes

Many of the beautiful and exotic feathers that were once standard materials in traditional salmon fly patterns are no longer available and today's tyer must compromise with substitute materials. To be honest, I cannot say that I regret this for in a few cases the scarcity of some materials is due to wise conservation planning. In other cases, particularly the birds of Africa and South America, the situation is much more serious. Their scarcity, I fear, has less to do with conservation than the wholesale destruction of the birds' natural habitat – the tropical rain forests. Naturally there will be many who would wish to tie a fly as near as possible to the instructions laid down by its inventor, and there is nothing wrong with this. Every good craftsman wants to do the job right, but personally I would much rather use substitute materials than to have on my conscience the thought that I had possibly contributed to the destruction of a rare and beautiful bird.

Following is a list of birds, the feathers of which you will come across in this book – some more frequently than others. I hope that you will find it interesting and helpful.

Domestic and Aviary Birds

Golden Pheasant

This brilliantly coloured bird originates from China where its name is 'Kinker' which signifies 'Golden-flower Fowl'. It is the bird used most frequently in the dressing of traditional salmon flies. The hen is dowdy and plain, but the strikingly handsome cock is able to provide parts for almost every fly. The golden-yellow crest feathers, commonly referred to as 'toppings', provide the tails for many flies when the shorter feathers are used. The longer toppings form part of the wings and are usually tied in over the main body of the wings. Some wings consist entirely of toppings, the 'Canary' being a good example.

Fibres from the bright orange and black 'tippet' feathers from the neck of the bird are used in the tails and wings of many flies. Often whole tippet feathers are used as 'under-wings', while in other flies such as the 'Rangers' the 'main' wings are made of them, and extremely nice wings they make too.

The scarlet 'sword' feathers found at the base of the tail feathers are occasionally used in the wings of some flies, e.g. Snowie's No. 1 pattern for the Garry of Loch Ness; the red feathers from the body of the bird (mainly the rump) can be used as hackles but are also used in wings, e.g. the 'Black and Yellow', while the most frequently used feathers are those from the long centre tail with their distinguished light and dark brown mottled pattern. Fibres from these feathers are used in the construction of so many 'married' wings that there seems little need to give an example.

It is unnecessary to search for substitute feathers as this bird is in plentiful supply, and bred by enthusiasts everywhere.

Guinea Fowl

In traditional salmon fly patterns this bird is more

often referred to as a Gallina (being a Gallinaceous bird), although the word is now more often spelt Gallena. It originates from the Western coast of Africa, principally towards the south, from the Cape of Good Hope as far as the coast of Guinea, from where it derives its name. Today the Guinea Fowl is a familiar farm-yard bird, being bred for its meat which tastes very similar to rabbit.

The rounded mottled neck feathers are often used as 'shoulder hackles', e.g. the 'Jock Scott' and the 'Blue Ranger', while other flies, for example the 'Colonel', have fibres from these feathers in their tails. Dyed bright blue, these neck feathers can also make a good substitute for Blue Jay.

The wing secondary feathers are occasionally used in the wings of some flies, e.g. Farlow's No. 1 pattern for the Oykel. Dyed a pinkish orange, the small neck feathers from the white variety of Guinea Fowl make a good substitute for the now rare Cock of the Rock.

Peacock

This fabulous bird was originally brought from India, and thence into Persia and Media. In the scriptures it is mentioned among the costly articles imported by the ships of Tarshish, employed by Solomon to enrich his country with the remarkable products of foreign nations.

The 'eyed' tail feathers of the cock bird provide the bronze herls which in some patterns are wound on as 'butts', e.g. the 'Judge', the 'McGildowny', and 'Powell's Fancy'. In a few other patterns like

Guinea Fowl

those for the Welsh Dee, bronze herls are wound on to form heads. The wings of one or two other flies contain a few bronze herls, while the 'Beauly Snow Fly' consists entirely of them.

From near the base of the Peacock's tail comes the unusual tapered feathers, with brilliant metallic-green herls, known as 'sword' or 'scimitar' feathers. These herls are featured more in sea trout flies than in salmon flies, and you may be familiar with that famous sea trout fly the 'Alexandra' which has wings of green Peacock herls. However, a few salmon flies occasionally use these herls in their wings or tails, e.g. Sir Alexander's No. 4 pattern for the Findhorn makes use of them in its wings.

The mottled wing secondaries are used in the wings of some flies – the No. 1 pattern for the Conon is a useful example. These feathers are often difficult to obtain, and when they are, buff mottled turkey tail is used as a substitute.

Turkey

In a domesticated state the plumage of the Turkey varies as much as the common poultry, and it is difficult to say which particular breed best provides the various feathers which are described. It is possible, however, to say that the white-tipped tails of the American Bronze variety are used in the wings of a number of flies like the 'Jock Scott' and the 'Toppy', but unfortunately, it can often be hard to obtain these feathers in good condition.

Other breeds provide the grey, and oak-brown speckled quill feathers, the latter making a good substitute for speckled Bustard (from the Great Bustard) and also the cinnamon feathers which are usually found on the rump of the bird, and the buff mottled tail feathers which provide the substitute for mottled Peacock wing. The birds providing the mottled feathers have become very scarce over the years due to their fall in popularity with breeders. The good news, however, is that you can now purchase substitutes which are produced by silk-screening the required pattern onto a common white Turkey feather. The results are amazing.

The fluffy feathers from the belly of the white Turkey provide the 'Marabou' which is used in a number of trout lures. Dyed grey or bright canary-yellow, Marabou makes a fair substitute for the leg feathers of an Eagle, which as you will rightfully assume, is used in the dressing of the 'Eagle'. The reddish dun feathers sometimes found in the bird's tail can be used as a substitute for 'Wild Turkey'; it is also used as a substitute for 'Gled', which is the name given to the Swallow Tailed Kite, and which, of course, is used in the dressing of the 'Gled Wing'.

White Goose

The wing coverts and the smaller shoulder feathers can be dyed scarlet to produce an excellent substitute for Scarlet Ibis. The wing secondaries are also useful for dying bright colours for use in the building of 'married' wings, although Swan is much more popular for this purpose.

Macaw

There are a few different kinds of Macaw, but the one used by the fly-tyer is the Blue and Yellow Macaw which originates from tropical America. This popular member of the Parrot family, and one of the best talkers, is common in aviaries throughout the world.

Fibres from its long blue and red tail are occasionally used in wings, but more usually it is the blue fibres which are used as *horns*. Dyed swan feathers make a fair substitute.

Wildfowl

Mallard

When in its winter plumage the drake provides us with the brown or bronze shoulder feathers which are much sought after. These feathers with their rickly streaked pattern are used in a good many patterns either as whole wings or to 'veil' over the main wings. Feathers referred to as 'grey drake' are the same feathers from the bird in its summer plumage.

Teal

The distinguished black and white barred feathers from the shoulder of the drake are much used in the wings of many flies, and occasionally in the tails. The 'Black and Teal' is an excellent fly which makes good use of Teal in its wings.

Widgeon and Pintail
Like the Teal, these ducks also have well marked black and white feathers that can be used for the same purpose.

Swan
There are few flies with 'married' wings which do not feature some Swan in them. The coverts and wing secondaries are ideal for wing building and are easy to dye. Although the Swan is a protected bird, you should have no trouble in acquiring feathers, at least in Britain, where the Swan is relatively common; a walk along the river bank or round your local park lake should produce enough feathers to keep you going for a while.

Shoveller Duck
This is the bird referred to as a 'Shovel' duck in the 'Britannia' pattern, which is the only one (at least in this book) which makes use of this bird. Its substitute is easily found in the Mallard which has a similar plumage.

Game Birds

Snipe
This is a useful bird to the dresser of trout and sea trout flies, but is of little importance to the dresser of salmon flies. I have mentioned it here only because the 'Major' carries a snipe feather in its wings.

Pheasant
Here I refer to the more common variety of Ring-necked Pheasant (*Phasianus colchicus*) which is to be seen in most parts of the British countryside. The tail feathers from both the cock and the hen occur in the wings of one or two flies, e.g. the 'Black Joke' has cock pheasant in its wings.

The white ring-neck feathers of the cock can be dyed to provide substitutes for Indian Crow and Toucan. The hen pheasant is able to provide a substitute for Bittern.

Partridge
The partridge I refer to here is the English, or Grey Partridge, not the French Partridge which is often used for the wings of Mayflies. The speckled silvery neck feathers are occasionally used as shoulder hackles. In one or two dressings black Partridge is given; this refers to the dark feather from the back of the bird – not a separate species.

Grouse
There are two species of Grouse found in Britain – the Red Grouse and the Black Grouse, both being similar in shape and size. Unfortunately Mr Francis does not tell us which particular bird was used in the dressings which contain grouse, so you have a choice. The speckled wing coverts and the hackles are used at the 'shoulders' of the occasional fly, e.g. Sir Herbert Maxwell's No. 1 pattern for the Luce.

Exotic and Rare Birds

Argus Pheasant
This spectacular bird is found in the mountains of central Malaya and central Annan where it is a secretive bird, haunting the high damp jungle. Its wings are poorly adapted for flight and the secondary quills are, in fact, three times longer than the primary, which spread out broadly at their extremities forming a large, sweeping, fan-like plume. Each of these feathers is beautifully ornamented with a row of eyes down the web on the outer side of the shaft, making it easy to understand why the bird was named after Argus the giant, who according to Greek mythology, had one hundred eyes. Its tail too is an amazing feature reaching up to 5 feet in length and 6 inches in width with a beautiful and complicated pattern of white and chestnut spots on a grey background. It is the fibres from the tail feathers, and the tips of the wing secondaries that are featured in the wings of a number of flies; the 'Blue Doctor' and the No. 3 pattern for Killarney and the Flesk are perhaps good examples.

Alas, I know of no really good substitute but a grey mottled Turkey tail with a few white spots painted on it might suffice.

Himalayan Pheasant
Nos. 4 and 5 of Mr Nicholay's patterns for the Shannon feature Himalayan Pheasant in their tails. It is difficult to define exactly which species Mr Nicholay refers to as there are in fact ten species

of Himalayan Pheasant with many sub-species known as 'kalijis', 'Silver Pheasants' and 'Firebacks', which are found from the Himalayas to China and Malaysia, where they live in forests at high altitude. However, I feel fairly certain that the bird in Mr Nicholay's patterns is a species known as the Impeyan Pheasant.

It is difficult to form an adequate idea of this beautiful bird, for the greater proportion of its plumage is dazzling with changing hues of steel-blue, green, violet, and golden-bronze. The bird looks as if it were clothed in a scale-armour of iridescent metal, while the feathers are soft and velvety to the touch.

Mr Nicholay advises that a topping dyed red makes an ideal substitute.

Blue Chatterer

This brilliant metallic-blue bird, about the size of a Starling, is found in the forests of central and northern South America, as is the Toucan, the Indian Crow, the Scarlet Ibis, and the Cock of the Rock which is a relative of the Chatterer. Once the Blue Chatterer's feathers were fashionable as salmon fly 'cheeks', but this beautiful bird is now rare and its place has been taken by the Kingfisher.

Cock of the Rock

This bird, about the size of a Jackdaw, has a plumage of bright orange with black wings and tail. The male and female differ in that the male carries a helmet-like crest which conceals its bill. The female builds a nest of mud and vegetable fibre

Argus Pheasant

high on a rock-face deep in the jungle where it lays two eggs; but the male is a lazy bird and takes no part in nesting. The orange body feathers are chiefly used as 'sides' in wings, e.g. the 'Parson'. The exception is perhaps the 'Dovey Captain' which has Cock of the Rock feathers wound on as hackles at each joint of its body.

The small neck feathers from a white Guinea Fowl make a good substitute when dyed a pinkish orange.

Scarlet Ibis
This exotic bird, about the size of a Raven, is yet another which today's fly-tyer is unable to include in his shopping list. Fibres from its deep red plumage are used extensively in the tails of flies, e.g. the 'Candlestick Maker' and the 'Britannia'. Substitutes are easily produced by dying the wing coverts of a white Goose scarlet.

Indian Crow
This small black bird with a striking red head and breast is, in fact, unconnected with India; it is the Red-ruffed Fruit Crow of Venezuela and Colombia. The red breast feathers are used in quite a number of flies like the 'Blue' and 'Black Ranger' and the 'Jock Scott' which have them in their tails. Other flies like the 'Popham' and, as its name would no doubt suggest, the 'Indian Crow', use them to great effect to 'veil' over their bodies.

This is another rare bird which is no longer available, but a good substitute can be had by

Cock of the Rock

dying the white 'ring-neck' feathers from a common cock Pheasant.

Toucan

You don't have to be a 'Guinness' drinker to know what this bird with its massive banana-like beak looks like; the brewers of this celebrated stout have made the Toucan familiar to all from their advertisements.

The yellow-orange breast feathers are used to 'veil' over the bodies of flies in the same way as Indian Crow feathers. The 'Jock Scott' would never be the same fly without the Toucan feathers which 'veil' over the yellow part of its body.

Like the rest of the exotic South American birds, it is almost impossible to acquire, but just like the Indian Crow a good substitute is produced by dying the white 'ring-neck' feathers from a common cock Pheasant.

Wood Duck

This bird, which is often called the 'Summer Duck', is a native of northern U.S.A. and Canada. It was once numerous, but today it is impossible to obtain. Its beautiful black and white barred feathers were once an important feature in the wings of many salmon flies. Now, however, we must make use of a substitute. Fortunately the Mandarin Duck has similar feathers amongst its plumage which, although not exactly the same, makes a reasonable substitute.

Wood Duck

Jungle Cock

The Sonnerat's Jungle Fowl is to be found in the jungles of north-east India and Assam and is about the size of a small Bantam Cock. The cock birds were once sought after for their magnificent capes (neck feathers) which consist of black feathers with white markings in the centre and a yellow-orange 'eye' at the tip which looks as though it has been touched on with a high-gloss enamel paint.

The governments concerned have now made it an offence to export these birds in the interest of their conservation, and who could argue with such a wise decision? Because of this the Jungle Cock can only be supplied by an enthusiastic breeder – if you happen to know of one – and a few do exist.

However, you must be prepared to pay a King's ransom for a full cape.

I have mentioned Jungle Cock substitutes earlier in my instructions on how to dress a salmon fly. But it might be worth mentioning that an American manufacturer is now producing substitutes by photographically reproducing 'eye' feathers onto a thin flexible plastic sheet. You can hardly tell them from the real thing.

Great Bustard (Otis tarda)

A large bird which is found in south-eastern Europe, although it was once an inhabitant of Salisbury Plain where in recent years attempts have been made to re-introduce it. Its speckled brown wing feathers were used in the wings of many flies and also as shoulder hackles, e.g. the 'Major'. This is one more bird which is also unobtainable. The best substitute is perhaps an oak brown mottled Turkey feather.

Florican Bustard (Otis aurica)

This relative of the Great Bustard is found in India and is similar in size, which is about the same as a Turkey. The wing feathers are used in some 'built' wings and serve to enhance the appearance of such flies as the 'Priest', the 'Switching Sandy' and the 'Laxford', to name but a few. They are barred in three shades of brown, being buff, cinnamon, and dark brown. I know of no readily available substitute and my suggestion is to mark a Swan feather with felt-tip pens.

Flamingo

My reason for mentioning this familiar bird is that it is featured in Mr Nicholson's No. 5 pattern for Galway and Connemara. The feather used in this pattern is a small pink feather from the breast of the bird, and a substitute is easily made by dying the breast feather from a Swan pink. Failing that you will find that most wildfowl reserves keep a few Flamingoes and a visit to one of these establishments could be very rewarding. Incidentally, I once tied a salmon fly with pink Flamingo wings from a feather which I picked up at Martin Mere, which is a centre belonging to the Wildfowl Trust. I killed three salmon on this fly before it got hooked up on the rocky bottom of the River Tummel.

Ostrich

Although it is not a rare bird I have included it here as, like the Flamingo, it may possibly qualify as an exotic one. It lived originally in the grasslands and semi-desert of Africa, but because of its commercial value to the fashion trade it has been farmed, and sometimes liberated, in other parts of the world, such as Australia and South America.

The fluffy herls from the plumes of this giant, flightless bird are used to form the 'butts' of the majority of flies. I have occasionally deviated from the original patterns when tying the 'Doctors' by using red Ostrich herl instead of crewel.

Blue Jay

When following patterns it is important that you do not confuse this bird with the more common British Jay. The Blue Jay is an exotic bird peculiar to North America where it inhabits the deepest recesses of the forest. It is about the same size as the British Jay but with a much longer tail. It has a black collar and a white throat and belly, while its greater wing coverts and tail are a brilliant turquoise-blue. It is these blue feathers which were used, particularly as 'shoulder hackles', in a great many flies, but today they are very scarce indeed. Dyed bright blue the rounded mottled neck feathers from a Guinea Fowl make a good substitute. Alternatively, you can use the blue wing coverts of the common Jay, particularly in smaller flies.

Blue Jay

Swallow-Tailed Kite (Gled)
Feathers from the long forked tail of this bird are featured in one or two patterns, the 'Gled Wing' itself being the best example. On rare occasions this bird has been sighted in Britain but it is more common to the southern States of North America from where it migrates to Brazil and Colombia. The forked tail which is characteristic of Kites reaches its greatest development in this bird. It is not to be confused with the British Red Kite which is now rare and confined to the sessile oak country of mid-Wales. It may be interesting to note that perhaps less than three hundred years ago the Red Kite was a common sight as it soared about London Bridge in great numbers. The Gled, or Swallow-Tailed Gled, is the Old English name for the Kite.

You will find it very difficult to obtain feathers from this bird, but reddish dun turkey feathers or similarly dyed Swan feathers make good substitutes.

Wild Turkey
Sir Herbert Maxwell's No. 1 pattern for the Luce has wings of red Wild Turkey, which is my reason for saying something about the bird here. It is thought that the domestic Turkey is descended from the Wild Turkey of Virginia which was the favourite feast of early settlers there; and hence the verse:

> 'Turkeys, carps, hoppes, piccarel, and beer,
> Came into England all in one year,'

You would be extremely lucky to obtain Wild Turkey feathers, but reddish dun Turkey tail feathers from the domestic kind make a good substitute. Alternatively, a Swan feather dyed the same shade is equally as good.

Other (British) Birds

Kingfisher
The brilliant turquoise-blue feathers from the back of this beautiful bird are used for 'cheeks' in almost every fly which has them. Originally the Blue Chatterer was the favourite for this purpose but as it became more and more scarce, the Kingfisher came more into use as its substitute. Of course, the Kingfisher is rightfully protected in Britain but imported birds can still be purchased, although as a conservationist I must confess that I find the sale of these imported birds disturbing, to say the least. A very good substitute can easily be made by dying suitably small white feathers the appropriate shade of blue.

Heron
This bird is another which now enjoys protection in Britain. Its long hackles are the very thing for many of the 'Dee' flies like the 'Tartan' and the 'Gled Wing' for instance. Unfortunately I know of no really suitable substitute for the Heron. However, it should not be too difficult to pick up a few feathers round a heronry, or alternatively, you could ask a friendly gamekeeper to keep his eye open for some.

Bittern
This shy and uncommon bird is also protected. My reason for mentioning it is because a very small number of patterns make use of it; the 'Bittern' itself perhaps being the best example. The best substitute is probably made from a hen Pheasant's wing by staining it a pale yellow. The black bar is then marked in with a felt-tip pen.

Common Jay
With all due respect to the Jay, I use the word 'common' simply to distinguish it from its American cousin, the Blue Jay. The lesser wing coverts of this bird are striking feathers in contrast to the rest of its plumage, having on them white and black stripes on a brilliant blue background. These blue feathers are mainly used as shoulder hackles, but because the fibres are rather short they are often tied in over a 'primary' shoulder hackle. Should longer fibres be required, however, the rounded speckled neck feathers of the Guinea Fowl dyed the right shade of blue will make a reasonable substitute, as it does for the Blue Jay. Some writers give complicated instructions for splitting the stalk so that the feather can be wound on as a hackle. My advice is not to bother – it can drive you mad! It is so much easier to simply tear off the amount of fibres which you require and tie them in as a false hackle. The fly will look just as

good, if not better, and moreover, you will have less trouble when you come to tie in the wings.

Golden Eagle
This great bird of prey, with its magnificent flight, is now seldom seen except in the north of Scotland, although in recent years it has made a return to the English Lake District where its nest site is kept a strict secret. The plumage is dark brown, with golden brown on the head and nape. Today this rare bird is protected by law. However, the Victorians had no misgivings about hunting it, believing in their ignorance that the Eagle was responsible for carrying away many lambs, and even the odd child. Consequently, it is not too surprising that the Eagle's feathers became the ingredients of one or two salmon flies. See under 'Turkey' (Marabou) for substitute.

AND SO FAREWELL

Drawing to a close is perhaps comparable to the end of an enjoyable day's fishing, when the sun is sinking beyond the distant hills and the temptation to stay and fish through the night for sea-trout is a strong one. But, really we know that the time has come to leave and reluctantly the line is finally reeled in and we wend our way homeward along the bank. We reach the bridge where we take one long last look at the river, breathe a silent sigh of farewell, and turn for home.

And so, it is not without a twinge of regret that I reach the end of this book, for working on it was indeed a pleasure. Sorting out all the patterns into an order which I hope you will be able to follow easily was not without its headaches, but nevertheless I learned much by undertaking it. The artwork too was not without its problems, for I am not a gifted artist as so many of my more fortunate fellow beings can claim to be, and although the task was one of trial and error, it still remained a labour of love. I can only hope that my illustrations will be of some help to you when tying the various flies in this collection and that you will derive as much pleasure from tying them as I did from working on this book.

I now leave you with some words of advice from Francis Francis which are to be found within the pages of his work *A Book on Angling*, as I think it is only fitting that the last words should belong to him.

> Depend upon it, brother angler, that there is no dogmatic rule to be laid down either for maidens or fish. Take the word of one who hath had experience of both. You can't diagram them; you must study their humours as well as you can, and suit your arts to your customer as near as may be. If that fails, try perseverance.

Index of Flies

Plate numbers are printed against patterns that are illustrated in colour. The symbol ☆ denotes patterns that are illustrated in black and white in the text.

GENERAL FLIES

The Blue Doctor (Plate 1) 1
The Silver Doctor 1
The Colonel (Plate 1) 1
The Major 2
The Black Ranger 2
The Blue Ranger 2
The Parson (Plate 1) 2
The Butcher (Plate 1) 3
Fin's Butcher 3
The Baker 3
The Candlestick Maker 4
The Childers 4
The Claret 4
The Black and Teal☆ 4
The Namsen 5
The Popham (Plate 1) 5
The Britannia 5
The Goldfinch 6

FLIES FOR SCOTTISH RIVERS

The Tweed
The Durham Ranger (Plate 2) 7
Jock Scott (Plate 2) 7
The Dun Wing 8
The Drake Wing☆ 8
The White Wing 8
The White Tip 8
The Toppy 8
The Black and Yellow 9
The Wilkinson 9
Sir Richard (Plate 2) 9

The Kirkcudbrightshire Dee
Mr Laurie's pattern 9

The Cree and its tributary, the Minnick
(Sir Herbert Maxwell's patterns)
No. 1 10
No. 2 10
No. 3 10

The Bladenoch
Notes on the Bladenoch and its flies 10

The Luce
(Sir Herbert Maxwell's patterns)
No. 1 10
No. 2 10
The Dusty Miller 11

The Ayrshire Stinchar
Notes on the Stinchar and its flies 11

The Annan and Nith
(Mr Rowell's patterns)
No. 1☆ 11
No. 2 12
No. 3 12
No. 4 12
Jamie Wright's pattern 12

Aberdeenshire Dee
The Gled Wing (Plate 3) 13
The Tartan (Plate 3) 13
The Eagle (Plate 3) 14

The Don
(Mr Brown's patterns)
No. 1 14
No. 2 14
No. 3 15
No. 4☆ 15
No. 5 15
No. 6 15

The Deveron
Notes on the Deveron and its flies 15

The Ness
No. 1 16
No. 2 16
No. 3 16
No. 4 16
No. 5 16
No. 6 17
No. 7 17
The Denison (Plate 4) 17
The Highlander 17

The Garry of Loch Ness
(Mr Snowie's patterns)
No. 1 18
No. 2 18
No. 3 18
The Snow Fly (Plate 4) 18

The Conon
No. 1☆ 19
No. 2 19
No. 3 19

The Lochy
(Mr Farlow's patterns)
No. 1 20
No. 2 20
No. 3☆ 20
No. 4 20

The Thurso
The Dhoon Fly (Plate 4) 21
The Duke of Sutherland 21
Sir Francis Sykes 21
The Priest☆ 21
Switching Sandy 22

The Laxford
(Mr Farlow's patterns)
The Laxford 22
The Lascelles☆ 22

The Awe and the Orchy
(Colonel Campbell's patterns)
The Canary (☆) 23
The Indian Crow 23
The Colonel's Butcher 24

(Mr Macnicol's patterns)
No. 1 24
No. 2 24
No.3 (☆) 24
No. 4 25
No. 5 25
No. 6 25

The Shin
(Mr Snowie's patterns)
No. 1 25
No. 2 25
No. 3(☆) 26

The Oykel
(Mr Farlow's patterns)
No. 1 (☆) 26
No. 2 27
No. 3 27

The Brora
(Mr Snowie's patterns)
No. 1 27
No. 2 27
The John Scott (☆) 27

The Helmsdale
(Mr Snowie's patterns)
No. 1 28
No. 2 28
No. 3 28

The Beauly
(Mr Snowie's patterns)
No. 1 28
No. 2 29
The Beauly Snow Fly (Plate 5) 29

The Findhorn
(Sir Alexander Cumming's patterns)
No. 1 (☆) 30
No. 2 30
No. 3 30
No. 4 30
No. 5 31
No. 6 31
No. 7 31
No. 8 31

The Tay
(Mr Paton's patterns)
The Black Dog (Plate 5) (☆) 32
The Claret Wasp 33
The Black Wasp 33
The Blue Wasp (Plate 5) 33
The Tay Tartan 33
The Royal (Plate 5) 34
The Scottish Shannon 34

(Mr Anderson's patterns)
The Yellow Wasp 34

The Dunkeld☆ 34
The Lord James Murray 35
The Fancy Olive 35
The Plain Shannon (Plate 5) 35

The Tummel, Garry and Isla
(Patterns from Pitlochry)
No. 1 36
No. 2 36
No. 3 36

The Lyon
No. 1 37
No. 2 37
No. 3 37

The Earn
(Mr Paton's patterns)
No. 1 Wasp☆ 37
No. 2 Wasp 37
No. 3 Wasp 37
(Other unnamed patterns)
No. 1 38
No. 2 38
No. 3 38
The Olive 38

The Teith
(The Hon. W. Drummond's patterns)
No. 1 38
No. 2☆ 38
(Mr Cameron's patterns)
No. 1 39
No. 2 39
No. 3 39
No. 4 39

The Forth
Notes on the forth and its flies 39

The Spey
The Spey Dog☆ 40
The Purple King (Plate 5) 40
The Green King 40

Loch Lomond
No. 1 41
No. 2 41
No. 3 41
No. 4 41
No. 5 42
No. 6 42
No. 7 42
No. 8 42
No. 9 42
No. 10 42
No. 11 42
No. 12 42

FLIES FOR IRISH RIVERS AND LOUGHS

The Erne
Notes on 'The Parson' 43
(Mr Rogan's patterns)
No. 1 44
No. 2 44
No. 3 44
No. 4 44
No. 5 The H.I.S. 45

Lough Melvin
(Mr Rogan's patterns)
No. 1☆ 45
No. 2 45
No. 3 45
The O'Donoghue (Plate 6) 46

Lough Gill
The Lough Gill Fly☆ 46

The Moy
The Thunder and Lightning (Plate 6)☆ 46
The Orange and Grouse 47
No. 1 47
No. 2 47
(Mr Hearns' patterns)
No. 3 48
No. 4☆ 48
No. 5 48

Lough Conn
(Mr Hearns' patterns)
No. 1 48
No. 2 48
No. 3☆ 49

The Owenmore and Ballycroy Rivers
The Owenmore (Plate 6) 49
An unnamed fly 49
A killing pattern from H.I.S.☆ 50
A second pattern from H.I.S. 51
A pattern from Mr Hearns 51

Galway and Connemara
(Mr Nicholson's patterns)
No. 1 51
No. 2 51
No. 3 52
No. 4 52
No. 5 52
No. 6 52
Mr Macredy's fly☆ 52

Lough Inchiquin
The Inchiquin☆ 53

The Lennan and Lough Fern in Donegal
Notes on the river, lough and flies 53

The Shannon
The Shannon (Plate 6) 53
(Mr Nicholay's patterns)
No. 1 54
No. 2 54
No. 3 54
No. 4 54
No. 5 55

Killarney and the Flesk
No. 1☆ 55
No. 2 55
No. 3 56
No. 4 56

The Laune
No. 1 (Plate 6) 56
No. 2 56
No. 3 57

The Lee, Cork
The Yellow Anthony☆ 57
The Orange Anthony 57
(Mr Haynes' patterns)
No. 1 57
No. 2 58
No. 3 58
No. 4 58
No. 5 58
No. 6 The Spider☆ 58

The Cork Blackwater
(Mr Haynes' patterns)
No. 1☆ 59
No. 2 59
No. 3 59

The Bandon
(Mr Haynes' patterns)
No. 1 60
No. 2☆ 60
No. 3 60
No. 4 60
No. 5 61
No. 6 61

The Caragh and Lough Currane
(Mr Haynes' patterns)
No. 1 61
No. 2 61
No. 3☆ 62
No. 4 62

The Kerry Blackwater
No. 1 62
No. 2 62
No. 3 62

The Suir
(Mr Staples' patterns)
No. 1 63
No. 2 63
No. 3 63
The Mystery 63
The Crane☆ 64
The Old Blue (Plate 6) 64
The Blue and Orange 64

The Nore
(Mr Staples' patterns)
No. 1☆ 65
No. 2 65
No. 3 65
No. 4 65

The Bush
(William Doherty's patterns)
The Butcher Fly 66
The Judge☆ 66
The McGildowny 66
The Erly 66
(Mr Farlow's patterns)
Powell's Fancy 66
The Grace☆ 67

The Bann
(William Doherty's patterns)
The Garibaldi Fly☆ 67
The Golden Olive Fly 68
The Green Grouse 68
The Blue Jay 68

FLIES FOR WELSH AND ENGLISH RIVERS

The Usk
Berrington's Favourite☆ 69
Francis's Favourite (Plate 7) 70
The Hornets 70
(Mr Crawshay's patterns)
No. 1☆ 70
No. 2 70
No. 3 70

The Wye
(Captain Hotchkiss' patterns)
The Bittern (Plate 7) 71
No. 1 71
No. 2 71
No. 3 71
No. 4 71
No.5☆ 71
No. 6 72

The Dovey or Dyfi
The Welshman's Fairy (Plate 7) 72
The Dovey Captain 72

The Conway
(Mr Blackwall's patterns)
The Blackwall (Plate 7) 73
No. 1 73
No. 2 73
No. 3☆ 73
No. 4 74

The Cothi
(Mr Harrison's patterns)
No. 1 74
No. 2 74
Mr Benyon's pattern☆ 74

The Taff
(Mr Benyon's patterns)
The Trewern Tickler☆ 75
No. 1 75
No. 2 75
No. 3 75
No. 4 75

The Tivey or Teifi, and Towy
(Colonel Lewes' patterns)
The Black Joke (Plate 7) 76
The Saville 76
Cock of Heullan Falls 76
The Captain (Tivey) 76
The Colonel (Tivey) 77
The Golden River Fly (Plate 7) 77
Mr Pryse's pattern☆ 77
Morgan's Fly (Plate 7) 77

The Dee
(Colonel T's patterns)
No. 1 78
No. 2 (Plate 7) 78
No. 3 78
No. 4 78

The Esk
(An old miner's patterns)
No. 1☆ 78
No. 2 79
No. 3 79
No. 4 79

The Eden
(Mr Rowell's patterns)
The Chimney Sweep (Plate 8) 79
No. 1 80
No. 2 80
No. 3☆ 80
No. 4 80

The Lune
(Mr Naylor's patterns)
No. 1 81
No. 2 81
No. 3 81
No. 4 81
(Mr Parker's patterns)
No. 1☆ 81
No. 2 82

The Ribble and Hodder
(Mr Pritt's patterns)
The Ramsbottom's Parson (Plate 8) 82
The Yellow and Scarlet Mallard 82

The Ribble and Hodder (continued)
(Mr Pritt's patterns)
The Green Mallard (Plate 8) 82
(Mr Ramsbottom's patterns)
The Cinnamon☆ 82
The Winesop Black (Plate 8) 83

The Tyne
(Mr Cook's patterns)
No. 1 83
No. 2 (Plate 8) 83
No. 3 84
Mr Robson's pattern☆ 84

The Taw and Torridge
(Mr Farlow's patterns)
No. 1 84
No. 2 (Plate 8) 84
No. 3☆ 84